the coolcamping guide to

FESTIVALS

Sam Pow

The Cool Camping Guide to Festivals
First edition published in the United Kingdom in 2009 by
Punk Publishing Ltd
3 The Yard
Pegasus Place
London
SE11 5SD

www.punkpublishing.co.uk

ISBN: 978-1-906889-00-5

10 9 8 7 6 5 4 3 2 1

introduction

As the year rolls forward, days get longer and the sun edges out from behind wintery clouds, we tentatively emerge from our sleepy hibernation, awakened by the promise of an exciting new festival season. Some readers will have been planning their festival itinerary since the day they threw out the Christmas tree, itching for the advent of warm weather and all the fun it brings. But for the thousands of you still making up your minds about what to do this or next year, let this book be your guide.

Why are we so fond of festivals? Aside from the obvious reasons — feeling the grass between our toes, watching our favourite bands, immersing ourselves in fantasyland while savouring the sweet taste of outdoor freedom — probably the biggest pull is the opportunity to escape the daily grind. And because we are innately social creatures at heart, the opportunity to mingle with like-minded souls, whether they share our love of the arts, for food or for dressing up, is now easier than ever thanks to the hundreds of festivals willing our custom. But which to choose?

This book offers a hand-picked selection of festivals in the UK and Europe that caters for all tastes and ages. Whether you're after the huge, household-name giants, the best in cultural events, the boutique festivals *du jour*, or just a small, idyllically located camping weekender, we've covered a collection that is sure to have you digging out your tent this instant.

To make your decision easier we've categorised the 50 festivals into '5 festivals good for...' anything from hedonism through to historical settings. We offer features on the best festivals to take kids to, celebrate environmental values or to hear new bands. A collection of 'Insider Insights' reveal special memories and glimpses of the festival world through the eyes of seasoned festie-heads who've made their own marks on the scene over the years. And Emily Eavis offers an exclusive perspective on her most memorable 10 Glastonbury festivals.

Festivals have come a long way over the years (take a look at the Timeline, p6) and are now so ingrained in the British psyche they've become as much a part of our summer culture as Wimbledon, Pimms and lemonade, the Notting Hill Carnival and strawberries and cream...So to satisfy your fervent festival ardour, with no further ado, we wish you the best season, ever!

festivals timeline

1947 The first ever Edinburgh International Festival. Several theatre companies arrived hoping to perform, only to be turned down. They set up the 'Fringe', which is now the biggest performing arts festival in the world.

1967 The Monterey International Pop Music Festival was America's first seminal festival. Awash with Californian, bohemian peace and love, the three-day spectacular saw Jimi Hendrix set fire to his guitar, a set by Otis Redding (who died later that year) and British group The Who win over a new American fan base.

The second 'summer' of love – a term loosely applied to two or three seasons of unlicensed rave parties. Music and nightlife were moving outdoors.

1992 The infamous, free, week-long Castlemorton Common Festival at Great Malvern, Herefordshire was so over-subscribed it made front page headlines, marking the downfall of outdoor rave culture and hastening the introduction of the Criminal Justice and Public Order Act.

1996 The Stone Roses played their final ever gig at Reading and the new V festival, V96, was launched – headlined by Pulp. The same year saw David Bowie, Björk and Nuyorican Soul wow audiences at the short-lived Phoenix Festival, outside Stratford.

2000 A new dance site at Glastonbury, The Glade, was born, lit up rather magically in the upper fields. In 2005 it struck out as an independent festival in its own right, eventually moving out of its Berkshire base to roomier Hampshire ground in 2009.

1997 The great Glastonbury wash-out.

1969

The now legendary Woodstock celebrated idealistic values on farmland just outside New York. Richie Havens opened the event that featured Ravi Shankar, Janis Joplin, Joe Cocker and Neil Young. In December, the Rolling Stones organised their own American free festival (in Altamont).

1970

Glastonbury was born. The third Isle of Wight blues, folk and rock festival was attended by over half a million, mostly Jimi Hendrix, fans. A far cry from today's slick production, it featured small music stages and diabolical facilities and was thereafter banned by the council.

1988

Local actor, Peter Florence started the literary Hay Festival in 1988 with his poker winnings – a game that visiting Bill Clinton (who famously described the festival as 'The Woodstock of the mind') played all night long there in 2001.

1982

Peter Gabriel devised WOMAD as a global promotion of self-expression and celebration. It attracted 15,000 people to Shepton Mallet in its inaugural year. Since then there have been over 160 WOMAD festivals in more than 27 countries.

2002

Glastonbury installed a new £1 million fence devised to keep out non-ticket holders and to deter dangerous overcrowding. The entry fee had been gradually rising from its £1 launch price; this was the last year an adult ticket cost under £100.

2005

The great Glastonbury wash-out (part II).

2009

Big Green Gathering returns after a year off; a former WOMAD director launches free-entry Heavenly Planet festival; Glastonbury sells out in record time.

2003

The Big Chill ran two summer events – one as a farewell to its old site (5,000-capacity Larmer Tree Gardens) and another celebrating its new home, Eastnor Castle, a beautiful Herefordshire valley with a capacity for 35,000.

7

festivals at a glance

Now that festivals are such big business, if you dig deep enough dozens of small intimate events are taking place underground. For any start-ups that don't make it back the following year, you can bet your bottom dollar something similar will be going on somewhere in the UK.

Antic Banquet enjoyed a good start in 2008. A novel concept, the festival's quirk is in the name – after a weekend spent partying to meaty hip-hop, reggae, gypsy, ska and booming dubstep, everyone converged for a Sunday afternoon feast.

The collective behind the event is The Antic Establishment, a creative off-shoot of The Secret Garden Party (p98). The team staged their first Valley of the Antics in 2007 and then dived headfirst into organising their own Antic Banquet weekender the following summer.

Décor-wise, white picket fences, large cardboard cut-outs of animals, hay bales and deckchairs straining under neon-clothed 20-somethings manifested a pleasant, nu-medieval air to the proceedings. The site's main hangout was a grassy circle wide enough to host silly team games, and various workshops, bars and dance spaces provided the entertainment before everyone settled down for Sunday's banquet.

Feeding 500 sounds like a biblical task and a half, but the caterers coped admirably, spit-roasting two pigs and boiling pots of bean stew with military precision. After chopping up 50 lettuces, 20 red cabbages, 10 kilos of red onions and countless tomatoes, the 'performance art' salad was hoisted atop a mobile home roof, then thrown down onto a tarpaulin and drenched with buckets of dressing, before being tossed by many pairs of helping hands.

Not back on until 2010 (it's going biennial) the Antic Banquet moves to a new home in Norfolk, but the aesthetics will remain the same.

WHEN Early/mid September
GUIDE PRICE £62, including the feast.
CAPACITY 500, and for as long as it stays this small, the Sunday banquet will continue.
CAMPING Being such a small event you'll probably be parking, camping and partying without any need to walk too far between all three. Bell tents are available for hire, too.
TOP TIP This festival suits youthfully active, networking souls. If you do go, remember to take along your own plate and cutlery for the Sunday meal.

LIKE THAT, THEN YOU'LL LOVE
The Magic Loungeabout (www. themagicloungeabout.net) is also on next in 2010. It has well-known bands and a more family-focussed vibe.
LOCATION It's a secret but will be somewhere in Norfolk.

www.anticbanquet.com

Some of you may recall two Birmingham University graduates touting their ambitious business plan in the *Dragon's Den*. Their pitch? To gather 10,000 students in a Cornish coastal spot, play them reggae on a beach during the day, put riotous live acts on the main stage at night, serve off-licence-priced drinks and watch as the post-exam chemistry that turns most students into freshers-on-heat takes over.

Technology overlord Peter Jones was the only Dragon to recognise the potential of Celia and Ian's shared dream. But these budding entrepreneurs declined his offer, finding support from a holiday company, instead. After scouring the Cornish coast, they unearthed the picturesque Carruan Farm in Polzeath, which was the festival's base for the first two years. With a newly doubled capacity in 2009 they had to find a new home – a cliff-top location three miles from a beach is their new-found treasure.

Organisers conduct surveys before each event so that the line-up echoes the guests' preferred musical styles; cutting-edge, smaller breakthrough artists cover the more populist electro, dubstep, blues, soul and indie rock tastes. On top of the dozen stages, there are numerous *tiki* shacks, a huge 6,000-capacity club tent, an Ibizan sunset piña colada bar with panoramic views of the sea and mini yurts where jazz and ska bands play.

Everyone has to be off the beach by 9pm, but the bars in the festival arena stay open until the early morning. Groups head off to chill together in hot tubs in the Naked Sauna Area or warm themselves up in the incense-filled world music mezzanine. As an extra winning touch, student discounted meals cost just £3–5. Such a student-centric approach helps make Beach Break Live a memorable end-of-term blow-out – and the perfect way to complete your education.

WHEN Mid June (after exams)
GUIDE PRICE £84, don't forget your student ID – it's a requirement.
CAPACITY 10,000
CAMPING Campsites are named after surf breaks (Boobies, Sandymouth, Lustyglaze and Banjo). Flush students can hire beach huts with sea views,

posh loos and BBQ areas.
TOP TIP Don't rush home afterwards – now that you're in heavenly Cornwall, you may as well stay to surf, swim and party for as long as your student budget will stretch. For a cheap cool campsite, head to Porth Joke Campsite (www.treagomill.co.uk) near to

Newquay's beaches.
LIKE THAT, THEN YOU'LL LOVE The active watersports event Wakestock (www.wakestock.co.uk) in Abersoch, North Wales.
LOCATION A secret cliff-top site in North Cornwall.

www.beachbreaklive.com

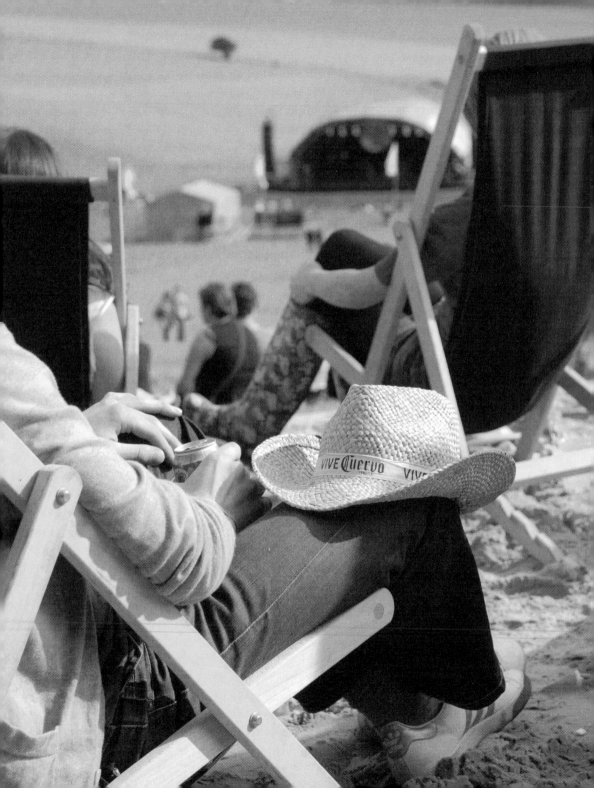

Brighton is a notorious playground for wild, party-loving hedonists (though, of course, some residents do choose quieter lives). Aside from the pubs, clubs and tasty restaurant grub, a rather fabulous beach awaits pebble skimmers and jet-skiers alike. And just down the road (a short bike ride away) are the breathtaking South Downs, boasting wind-blasting walking trails with fantastic sea views.

Why has it taken so long for anyone to recognise and make the most of Brighton's best assets by throwing a huge open-air party? Not since Brighton's memorable Essential festivals in the late-1990s has the city seen anything like an event on this scale.

Obviously, though, there's more to producing a successful festival than scoring a fabulous location. You need a cracking line-up, which Beachdown delivered in buckets and spades. You also need to incite masses of goodwill among your crowd. It was watching a mass exodus of their friends and neighbours leave for The Big Chill festival (p90) one year that spurred Joe Pidgeon and his business partner Darren Murphy into running their own event in the first place. Adhering to the most basic model of economics – the supply and demand theory – they quickly decided to give locals an event closer to home.

Once the organisers had convinced the local council that the site would be well looked after, Beachdown was in business. All they had to do next was tap into the huge market of festival goers who reside in the area and start selling tickets, which they did – in their thousands. And so, over the August bank holiday weekend in 2008, 10,000 people wended their way up on to the windswept South Downs, to the well-known area of natural beauty called the Devil's Dyke. Surrounded by rolling meadows this scenic landscape oozes rural countryside charm – even in the rain (for it did rain quiet hard at times that launch weekend).

A few shaky logistical hiccups were inevitable for a start-up venture of this size (and working against Mother Nature's elements, too). But on the whole, the crowd noticed only the music. Storming to the top of the festival charts, Beachdown's confidently programmed debut included a raft of home-grown bands and DJs, with stars such as Terry Callier, Fun Lovin' Criminals and Gogol Bordello adding international panache.

The organisers went to great lengths to ensure that the festival made a minimum impact on the environment. They used local businesses and traders and powered a fleet of shuttle buses with used cooking oil (see Eco-friendly Festivals, p136). And their strict Leave No Trace tidy-up policy meant that the council was satisfied enough to green-light future events.

Seasoned festival hands who are bored of eating the same old food that on the circuit won't find much to complain about here. Brighton is a city rich in gastronomic delights, so Beachdown was always going to go the extra mile to put on a scrumptious spread. Catalan tapas was dished up at the Pintxo People's food stall, Momma Cherri's soul food shack provided heaped portions to get everyone in the festive mood and the Sussex Yeoman served fabulous roasts, which were especially popular on the Sunday.

Beachdown's easy-going, intimate nature could be attributed to the crowd demographics; with so many locals here many of them already knew each other. Socially, Brighton isn't a city that's party-starved by any stretch of the imagination, but put a lively bunch like this in a field and there will always be fireworks. An increased capacity in 2009 will help to attract more out-of-towners, after all there's plenty of room up here. And if the indigenous tribes continue to slope off home to their own beds at the end of each night, it just means that there's always going to be more space for the remaining campers to enjoy.

Following its debut, Beachdown's production is sure to improve and it now has the potential to fill a huge eclectic festival void that has existed for far too long here on the south coast.

WHEN Late August. People are allowed onsite from Friday to Monday.
GUIDE PRICE £85
CAPACITY 15,000
CAMPING There are quiet and a noisy sections, so take your pick. You can hire beach huts, which are quite expensive, but they sleep two and are furnished with beds, curtains and even a kettle. Campsites are dotted around the site and because the South Downs sit on chalk in the earth, they won't turn into mud baths should it rain.
TOP TIP Don't pitch your tent outside of the camping areas on the slopes, because if it does rain you could find yourself sliding slowly down the hillside.
LIKE THAT, THEN YOU'LL LOVE Brighton Festival and Brighton Festival Fringe (www.brightonfestival.org) has been running for five decades and is the largest city arts event of its kind in England, with three weeks of theatre, dance, music (Afro-funk, world, gypsy bands), book, debate, children's and family shows taking over various venues in May.
LOCATION Beachdown, Dyke's Hill, Brighton, East Sussex BN1 8YJ

Beautiful Days

This colourful festival is the brainchild of the perennial festival band the Levellers and takes its name from one of their songs: 'What a Beautiful Day'. Having toured extensively as performers, the band has picked up the best tips on how to run a festival. No sponsorship, no branding and no adverts means organisers simply book who they like, regardless of an artist's chart position.

Judging by the acts that follow their own opening acoustic set, it seems that the Levellers have a penchant for folk, punk and roots, with splashes of dance music and comedy, thrown in.

Entertainment swerves the mainstream and isn't afraid of dipping into the past. The 'big' main stage bands of 2008 were Squeeze and Supergrass, while comedians ranged from the punk poet of John Cooper Clark to Richard Digance's gentle musical musings.

Most of the camping space is set slightly away from the entertainment arena, but at 12,500 capacity this is not a huge event, so you're never too far from any the excitement. And if you arrive early enough (gates open 9am on the Friday) you can nab a spot in the smaller campsite just a stumble away from the main arena. A big hit with families, the festival site is easy to negotiate and the Children's Area, where kids can slip into the pottery or circus skills classes, sits right in the middle.

There is no doubt that CAMRA (Campaign for Real Ale) would approve of the refreshments here – the local Otter Brewery runs the bars with pints at pub prices, including the festival's very own 'Beautiful Daze' brew on tap. Traditionally, at the end of the three days, the Levellers play a closing set to a reception akin to a hero's welcome. Beautiful days, indeed.

WHEN Late August
GUIDE PRICE Tickets are for weekend camping. Adult £100; 10–16 years £60; 5–9 years £30; and under-5s £5.
CAPACITY 12,500
CAMPING There are three main camping fields that all have showers, plus disabled facilities. The family camping area has story-telling and play areas for children.
TOP TIP Get yourself on the bill if you're a performer or artist, word is they treat their entertainers really, really well!
LIKE THAT, THEN YOU'LL LOVE The North Devon Festival (www. northdevonfestival.org), which takes place around about Barnstaple in June, features over 200 (mostly free) music, comedy and surf events.
LOCATION Escot Park, Nr Fairmile, Devon EX11 1LU

www.beautifuldays.org

beautiful days

Roll up, roll up festival mentalists. The Robin Hill Countryside Adventure Park near Newport on the Isle of Wight is a children's playground, with toboggan run, gypsy caravans, model village and giant rabbits. But come early September, these playful features fade into the background on the arrival of a colourful freak show.

Bestival didn't invent fesival fancy dress, but by encouraging the extreme efforts of their punters it might seem that way. Camping alongside cowboys, scuba-divers, Batmen and Robins or a pantomime horse is a blast and sets the scene for one hell of a weekend knees-up.

The festival's immediate success can be attributed to two things. Firstly, it knows its music; an area overlorded by the Radio 1 DJ Rob da Bank (see also p161). Secondly, it came along just as festival fever was exciting the masses, so its timing offered virgin festivallers inclusive membership to a club they could grow up with and call their very own.

The campsites look amazing, but Bestival is more about being outdoors in the action and only retiring to tents between parties. As for luggage, pack light. Who wants the bother of boiling a camping kettle when the Women's Institute tea tent is selling it for 60p a cup? After passing various eye-boggling goings-on on your way there, you'll probably want to start the day with something stronger instead, anyway.

In 2008 as a testament to the attitude of its fanbase, Bestivallers barely complained about the wet weather that would have terminally dampened most other festivals. That's what happens when 30,000 dressed-up loons refuse to let summer end without one last blow-out.

WHEN Mid September
GUIDE PRICE £140 adult (16s and over) weekend ticket; 13–15s £70; and 12s and under are free.
CAPACITY 30,000
CAMPING You can hire pods, bell tents, yurts and tipis (check website for details). The car parks are a hilly hike from the campsites, but that's a small price to pay for living it large in this splendid adventure playground.
TOP TIP A hardcore party mentality is vital, but if you need a break there's always the Restival area.
LIKE THAT, THEN YOU'LL LOVE Rock Ness (www.rockness.co.uk) in Scotland is an equally humungous party next to a beautiful loch with its own Bestival arena, aptly called Nesstival.
LOCATION Robin Hill Countryside Adventure Park, Downend, Nr Arreton, Isle of Wight PO30 2NU

www.bestival.net

CAMP Bestival

If the Daddy of the newer, hedonistic festivals is Bestival on the Isle of Wight, then Camp Bestival must be Daddy's illegitimate love child, banished across the seas to the mainland and told not to return to the white-cliffed Isle until he's all grown up.

But the likelihood of Camp Bestival ever growing up is as remote as a seven-year-old refusing ice cream, because this festival is definitely one for the kids.

Bouncing baby Bestival came into this world on the 18th of July 2008. Proud founder, Rob da Bank, had recognised that the original Bestival had a reputation for extreme hedonism and while this suited the hardcore elements, his plan was to create an alternative weekender with a more relaxed, family feel. Something your Gran could get as much enjoyment from as you. Of course, it would help if Granny was a fan of Kate Nash or DJ Yoda and was a dab-hand at putting up a tent.

Rob and the team worked hard to get the right balance of kid-friendly fun and traditional festival frolicking, and – aside from a few logistical problems like four-hour traffic queues on arrival and not enough loos or camping areas – the new kid on the block has succeeded in its transgenerational aims.

For the kids, a dedicated family field is transformed into a children's wonderland with hula-hoops, space-hoppers and crazy bikes scattered around, and clowns and redcoats on hand to make sure everyone's having just the right amount of fun. Sure-fire winners like bouncy castles, talent shows, a kids' disco and a dressing-up tent are supplemented with more unusual activities such as kids' yoga, mosaic making and the amazing Insect Circus.

But where Camp Bestival really succeeds is in thinking about those extras that make a parent's life easier: a dedicated toddlers' area, a breast-feeding tent, nappy-changing facilities and healthy kids' food. The family field even boasts a real-ale bar and half-decent music on the stage; it's all delightfully agreeable in a village-fête meets giant-kids'-birthday-party meets rock-star-wedding-reception kind of way.

So, that's the kids taken care of, what of the rest of it? Well, even the main festival area continues the family theme, with jousting, maypole dancing, marching bands and a pram park near the main stage. But this is 'Son of Bestival', so it's all about the music too, right? Well, yes and no. The inaugural Camp Bestival had some notable musical highlights including a crowd-rousing, high-energy performance by the Flaming Lips, a funky afternoon set from the Cuban Brothers and a masterful display of beat-box bravado from MC Beardyman. Curator Mr Bank is known for his all-inclusive, eclectic musical taste so you would expect the line-up at Camp Bestival to reflect that. But with such diversity, you're not going to please all the people all the time; there were rumblings about Chuck Berry being way past his prime and about the big weekend finale being a surprisingly low-key set from Kate Nash.

But hey, these are mere trifles in the context of a bumper weekend of fun and tomfoolery, of marching bands and happy camping, of tasty pies and Women's Institute cakes. And wasn't it lovely when the castle was lit up with blues and purples and greens against the night sky? Aaah!

So party people, parents and – yes – grannies too, come and enjoy all the cheeky, playful charisma of Bestival at this mainland, mainstream and firmly family-favourite spin-off.

Just think of Camp Bestival as an adorable baby, in those wonderful, heady years before it grows into a robust toddler, smears you with jam and jumps all over your stuff in the early mornings.

WHEN Late July
GUIDE PRICE Weekend tickets cost £130 per adult; £65 for 13–15s; and 12s and under go free.
CAPACITY 10,000
CAMPING As the title suggests, this is a haven for modern campers. Bring your own tent or hire one of the tipis, yurts, bivouacs, airstreams or gypsy caravans. There's parking right next to the campsites (due to overcrowding, many guests ended up having to 'camp' in the car park in 2008), plus hot showers, giant BBQs, a farmers' market and the local WI stall selling tea and cake.
TOP TIP Pack earplugs, of course!
LIKE THAT, THEN YOU'LL LOVE Camber Sands Holiday park (www. pontins.com/cambersandsholidaypark) is probably the next best thing for a similar full-on family adventure. In festival terms, take them to Glastonbury (p42) for an equally eye-popping experience. The kids' field there will amuse them for hours and everything else will stun them into silence.
LOCATION Lulworth Castle, East Lulworth, Wareham, Dorset BH20 5QS

www.campbestival.net

 creamfields

A shining beacon on the radar of most young dance fans, Creamfields is the longest established dance music festival in the UK and a touring success in no less than 13 countries, from Rio to Romania. Loud, proud and utterly anarchic, the UK festival is certainly not for the faint-hearted. It is little more than an extended full-on rave, a smorgasbord of house, trance and techno, where euphoria meets grime, funk meets bass and no one – and we mean no one – is shy about getting down and dirty.

The home of this 10 years-and-counting event is Daresbury, just 25 minutes from Liverpool and 45 minutes from Manchester. Obviously, it attracts a strong following from the north of England, not least from Liverpool where James Barton and Darren Hughes launched their now world-famous Cream nightclub back in 1992. Plenty of hardcore southerners make the pilgrimage up the M1 for the weekend, and the number of visitors from international lands increases in line with every new festival that Creamfields hosts abroad.

Saturday, at 9am, is when the fun begins. That's when eager ticket holders who've braved the queues early pile onto the site ready to set up camp for the duration. The camping compound is a recent addition at Creamfields. It has a large, open field well-equipped with burgers, beer and portaloos as well as a strong security presence. You can walk from here to the main arena in minutes, and there a welcoming contingent of cyber kids (yes, they do still exist) cheerily wave you in once the gates open at 2pm.

Saturday is the big rave day when all sorts of dance music gets an airing. Huge marquees featuring state-of-the-art production host drum 'n' bass to techno, trance, house, electro and everything in between. It's also the day to catch well-known headliners like Fatboy Slim, Underworld or The Prodigy on the main stage.

Rock back to the campsite as Sunday's dawn inches over the horizon, but don't expect sleep to be a priority. A large portion of campers never actually make it back inside their tents; the widespread 'carry on' mentality among these clubbers means they tend to continue making merry until the main arena reopens at midday. But if you really need your beauty sleep just be sure to pack some earplugs.

Sunday is a slightly more subdued affair. The outdoor stage is given over to commercial bands or non-dance-music acts (fashionable indie-rock-dance crossovers such as Ian Brown, Kasabian and Primal Scream). As the day progresses the atmosphere regresses towards the vibes of old that Creamfields regulars love and expect – marquees chock full of people giving it their all as the skies fill with a pyrotechnic display of coloured sparks. And the kind folks at Creamfields will let you stay one more night before kicking everyone off the site, and it's the wiser revellers that make the most of this generous opportunity to rest before wending their way home.

Grumbles about the UK's competing dance festivals are not uncommon; you're bound to hear frazzled, post-party moans berating anything from queuing systems and sound systems to the security, or comparing line-ups and the organisation with competing events. However, Creamfields is an experienced, professional international operation that's given thousands of ravers exceptional dancefloor joy and countless happy memories – even if some of those memories might be a little hazy.

Creamfields is very loud, utterly hedonistic and, most importantly, a lot of fun. Northern hospitality offers a cultural experience you're unlikely to forget. Expect glow sticks, silly outfits, cavernous laser-drenched marquees and hands in the air aplenty. Stick with your gang, and you'll have an unforgettable time.

WHEN Late August
GUIDE PRICE £115
CAPACITY 65,000
CAMPING New in 2008, a large green field opened to weekend ticket holders only. People bringing camper vans or caravans are directed to park up in the car park. As at most festivals, paid-for, luxury camping is available (podpads, Tangerine Fields etc.).
TOP TIP Start off at the festival with a drink in hand, indulging in some serious people watching – mad characters abound here. Giant furry boots, hair gelled into high peaks and aviator glasses are a few fashion staples paraded here.
LIKE THAT, THEN YOU'LL LOVE Creamfields in one of its international disguises. Creamfields Malta's (www. creamfieldsmalta.com) inaugural festival is one of its most recent foreign forays and was nominated for Best European Festival Award after being on the circuit for just one year. Now held over a local public bank holiday in August, boasting four arenas, and a line-up that's had a healthy cash injection, this Maltese party is one not to be missed.
LOCATION Daresbury, Halton, Cheshire

www.creamfields.com

Neon lights beckon through the trees, Cyndi Lauper's vocals play the Pied Piper, enticing festival guests towards the music – 'Girls just wanna have fun'! Two-dozen shadows are bouncing up and down on a raised disco floor.

An iPod sitting within a giant cardboard ghetto-blaster is a novel way of offering revellers control over what they can dance to, and everyone takes it in turns to pick one of the 400 songs. When we're done stomping over pink and orange squares we move deeper into the woods, where a crowd has gathered. There doesn't appear to be anything happening here. But then it comes into view: a piano, hidden in the trees. Someone steps up to the ivory keys and plays so magnificently that for some his performance was the musical highlight of the day.

But maybe they missed Richard Hawley, Two Gallants and Bon Iver. Three perfect examples of Eat Your Own Ears' exemplary music policy. Between them they presented smooth Sheffield sheen, shouty San Franciscan gloss and pensive Canadian charisma. A polite, attentive crowd studiously took in every movement, clapping on cue and pointedly staring at any late-comers disturbing the moment.

The Victorian pagoda by the main stage radiates in the setting sun, the resident peacocks and macaws are settling down for the evening and widespread veneration fills the air. We head towards the shop to check out the merchandise, but don't get far without stopping at the cider bus. There, a barely clothed man is swinging himself around a barrel, flashing a beaming smile and the odd bit of bum cheek as he does so (perhaps he'd had a little too much apple juice?). But it doesn't put anybody off joining the queue; sights like this simply add to the festival's jovial, laid-back atmosphere.

Back in the food field the top-end Bimble Inn tent stretches inwards like a tunnel. A low-level yurt fills up for the third and final night. At the bar a mother tells us how her sons enjoyed the break-dancing workshop and learning how to make animation characters out of plasticine.

We're dragged into The Big Top to see The Brakes. Despite the relentless rain that turned the earth into a muddy slurry on the first day, everyone has had a great weekend. The Brakes have played at End of the Road every year, and the fans express their love for their fast, literary short songs at high volume.

Just how did End of the Road become so successful? It seems that every UK festival has had to find a niche crowd to call its own, and the End of the Road has built its audience simply by slapping flyers at music venues the length and breadth of the UK. The festival is a melting pot for alternative-country, folk and bucolic bands, rockabilly swing, Scandinavian pop, punk rock (and post punk), blues, indie, baroque and lo-fi rock and is run without any corporate sponsorship or involvement; which is no mean feat in today's festival market.

Finding the venue is easy. Parking is a breeze. Just pick up tickets from the check-in booth, and you're in. Food stalls you don't normally encounter at other festivals are welcoming – a pile of North African spicy fish *bourek* (filo parcels) was dished up with a smile every bit as

hearty as the portion. There's plenty of seating, too, in various café tents, on logs and in the biggest tea garden that we've found at any event. This sedentary festival lifestyle ought to catch on; conversing over a cuppa makes a welcome change to mortgaging your soul in exchange for expensive cocktails and a torrent of funky house.

The bands attract the crowds here. Period. This is a mecca for *Rough Trade* subscribers, Camden bar crawlers, hip *Vice* magazine devotees and seasoned *Mojo* readers. Lopsided haircuts are common. Friendly-faced hearts beating with musical appreciation are even more so.

WHEN Mid September
GUIDE PRICE Adults and 13–16-year-olds pay £115 for a weekend ticket (including camping); it's £30 for 6–12s; 5s and under go free.
CAPACITY 5,000
CAMPING There are family and quiet areas, recycling bins, an Information Point, a no-noise (when neighbours are sleeping) policy and great landscape

vistas of Dorset countryside.
TOP TIP Keep an eye out for surprise turns by the main artists. You might find one of them DJing in a tent, playing piano in the woods or even strumming an acoustic guitar to an accompanying tune in the campsite.
LIKE THAT, THEN YOU'LL LOVE The Great Escape (www.escapegreat.com) in Brighton isn't a camping festival but

it has a similar knack for showcasing soon-to-be-huge new talent. Referred to as the UK's own SXSW (America's music industry convention – see Festivals For New Music, p161) it takes place in mid May and bills over 200 international bands in two-dozen music venues across the city.
LOCATION Larmer Tree Gardens, Donhead Saint Mary, Dorset SP5 5PY

www.endoftheroadfestival.com

FESTINHO

Bright flags, cocktails, BBQs, music and capoeira: Festinho celebrates all that is brilliant about Brazilian culture. Not just a barn-stomping party, it also raises money for charity ABC (Action for Brazil's Children Trust). By supporting this particular festival you'll be funding community-led projects that provide young, vulnerable Brazilian kids with training in acting, circus skills, art and music.

Festinho really is a labour of love. All of the organisers, stewards, staff and many of the artists give their time for free to ensure as much money as possible is fed directly to the charity.

Festinho began in 2005 in a very large back garden in Oxford, before moving to beautiful farmland within the Tudor outbuildings of Kentwell Hall, in Suffolk. The crowd is naturally amiable and super chilled. When bathed in sunlight, the green, white and yellow flags adorning the place create a scene to rival the best of Rio's beaches (ok, so indulge us here).

A main stage plays host to fantastic live acts such as The Bays, Hexstatic and Faze Action. But best of all are the timbered barns. One houses the main bar, opening onto an outdoor patio, below a covered dance space that rumbles with Brazilian funk. An arts and crafts exhibition

fills another old barn twinkles like a fairytale among the farmyard pig sheds and is filled with paintings, photographs, hand-crafted jewellery and screen prints (artists donate a percentage of any sales to the charity). Gas lanterns and glitter balls illuminate the grounds and the fir-tree woods where The Disco Shed pumps up the volume till the early hours.

Everyone who has been to Festinho is rooting for it to become the success it's worked so hard to be.

WHEN Late August/early September
GUIDE PRICE Adult weekend ticket £45, with camping £60; Sunday ticket £15. Under-14s free.
CAPACITY 2,000
CAMPING You'll be neighbours with the farm's horses, pigs and peacocks. Part of the campsite is nestled into the bottom of the woods, where there's a sauna and hot showers. A quiet camping area is sheltered by bushes, and live-in vehicles are (unusually for a festival) allowed in for free!
TOP TIP Festinho is a big, non-stop party, so to ease into the new day, head to the BBQ for a 'Brazilian hangover broth' (£1).
LIKE THAT, THEN YOU'LL LOVE Kent's Red List LIVE (www.redlistlive.com) aims to raise awareness of the IUCN's Red List of Threatened Species and money for The Aspinall Foundation. Five stages play rock to pop, indie to dance, in 600 acres of park next door to gorillas, elephants and rhinos at the Port Lympne Wild Animal Park.
LOCATION Kentwell Hall, Long Melford, Suffolk CO10 9BA

www.festinho.com

best 10y

at Glastonbury

Growing up hosting the UK's biggest festival in her back garden, Emily Eavis has played her own part in Glastonbury's evolution since the age of four. Today, as her father Michael's official lynchpin, she plays a key role in the festival's organisation and direction. Here she details her most memorable years.

1985 When I was little I'd go into denial that the festival was going on. I'd be like, 'Why doesn't everyone just go back to their own gardens?' That's why I was in the farmhouse living room, aged four, playing my violin. Then someone said, 'Wouldn't it be funny if Emily was on stage?' Within 10 minutes I was on my way to the Pyramid Stage. It was just before The Style Council and there was this massive crowd of about 40,000 people. I remember a stage hand shouting 'Dim the lights', and the whole audience was plunged into darkness. I wasn't actually nervous, cos I couldn't really see anyone and obviously you haven't really experienced nerves by the age of four. So I went onto the stage and played the only song I knew, which was 'Twinkle Twinkle Little Star'. I played it and then walked off and said, 'Mummy, my legs feel like jelly'. I couldn't

work out why they were shaking so much. Four or five encores later, the crowd were still going mad for it, while Paul Weller waited to go on. Unfortunately, my dad missed the whole thing because he was trying to talk a man down from a telegraph pole. He's really gutted about that.

1990 We usually steer away from hanging out backstage, but I did meet Shaun Ryder when I was nine because I was a big Happy Mondays fan. He literally fell on top of me and passed out, with me still underneath. I was like: that's cool, he didn't let me down; it's Shaun Ryder!

1993 I had to go into school on the Friday, because they were a bit funny about me missing days, but I remember getting home that afternoon and running down

the hill to the site, full of excitement. I just spent the whole weekend wandering around, taking it all in. That was the first year I really started to enjoy and appreciate it.

1995 We just had the best festival. It was so hot, I'd just finished my GCSEs, it was the first year I was allowed to camp and all my favourite bands were playing, particularly Oasis. That was the first time I sat around the campfire with people like Bez and Joe Strummer. I remember people were passing drugs around and I was so innocent to what it was that I just passed it on round the circle. At school, people assumed our family were crazy drug-takers or something, when it was actually quite the opposite. We're a very straight, conventional farming family really.

1997 I had my last A-Level exam the Thursday before this festival. Radiohead's set has gone down as one of the great Glastonbury moments. I think part of the reason that show was so magical is the fact that the rain was beating down. Suddenly their words, their music, all seemed perfect for that very moment. It just felt so dramatic. I've never seen a crowd so still. It was a really good festival, although that was also the year

that my dad told me Sting really wanted to play and I begged him to book him because my boyfriend was really into him. Sadly, he dumped me before the festival and then brought his new girlfriend along. I was heartbroken!

1999 My mum died a month before this festival. We had two choices: either cancel it or do it as a tribute to her. But she would've totally wanted it to happen. She was the backbone of the festival. As much as my dad has this amazing energy, she anchored him. So we went ahead with it and it was actually the most amazing tribute to her. The weather was beautiful and on the Sunday morning there was a minute's silence across the site. I remember I was a bit late, so I had to run out through the house and down into the Pyramid field. Everyone was standing outside their tents, just silent. It was an amazing thing to see. It felt like a shared moment. That one was definitely my most emotional festival, but in a really nice way. It was also the year when I started to become involved in the organising. It was a very natural thing; there was just such a gaping hole there without my mum. So I started working with my dad and it actually helped a lot with our grief. I've been helping out ever since, gradually doing more and more each year.

2000 This was the last year without the fence and there were rumours of 300,000 people being on site. Watching the Chemical Brothers on the Friday night on the Pyramid was the first time I'd ever felt scared during the festival. It was so packed it was frightening; which is why we took the next year off – to build the fence.

2005 Primal Scream have had some amazing Glastonbury performances over the years, but they managed to offend a few people backstage at this one and I had to intervene to stop them being chucked off the site. It was pretty full-on – my first serious showdown! But we've never, ever chucked anyone off the site, so I had to stop that happening. I'm happy to say it all worked out fine in the end though.

2007 The capacity was 15,000 bigger this year, so there had to be a new entertainment area and I really wanted to take it on, even though my dad wasn't sure I was ready. We came up with this field away from the main crowd bottlenecks, The Park. It was conceived as an area of calm and beauty, with bands you wouldn't find on the other stages. I always feel the pressure, but

I couldn't sleep this year. I really wanted it to be good. The weather made things difficult, but The Park went down really well.

2008 After the rain in 2007, I think some people were a bit fed up with Glastonbury, and suddenly everyone seemed to want to take a pop at it. We've never had as much criticism as we had before the 2008 festival and I've never felt so close to it all being over. We were attacked from all sides, and it became quite personal. Jay-Z's headline slot became a national debate; I remember turning on *Channel 4 News* and seeing Jon Snow saying, 'Is hip-hop wrong for Glastonbury?'. But throughout that time, the groundswell of support from our punters was getting stronger and stronger. By the time of the festival, we had this amazing hardcore of people who were determined to make it good. I cried when I saw everyone coming through the gates on the Wednesday morning. And then, of course, Jay-Z absolutely nailed it. It was definitely a big risk to book him, but all the other options were very obvious and uninspiring. And I'd rather go for something completely different – the best rapper in the world – than something under par. In the end it turned out to be the right decision. He gave the festival a whole new lease of life.

GLASTONBURY

Midsummer in the UK means one thing and one thing only. It's time to pack sunhats and wellies and head for the farm – Worthy Farm in Somerset to be exact. Every June, farm owner Michael Eavis transforms 900 acres into a miniature city. With the resident cows settled in a nearby barn, visitors from all over the world pile in for a long weekend of spiritual hedonism.

It's hard to think of a single event that's done more to rally the British into celebrating life with such wholehearted abandon. Falling in the path of ley lines that pass from the nearby Glastonbury Tor, the site flickers with a divine atmosphere that encourages all sorts of goings on. Equally important, the festival's involvement with the likes of CND and Greenpeace has always promoted political and charitable causes.

Pilton Festival, as it was called in 1970, attracted longhaired hippies who paid £1 in exchange for free milk (from the cows) and a headline performance by Marc Bolan. Die-hard fans have made an annual pilgrimage here ever since, witnessing the mutation from its pastoral folk-pop infancy into the colossal rock, iconic indie and turbo-powered dance music granddaddy of festivals it is today. Currently over 50 entertainment venues and a huge selection of side attractions make planning an itinerary nigh impossible.

Glastonbury's more recent moniker, 'Festival of Contemporary Performing Arts', has meant a flow of comedians, cabaret and theatre actors now take to the stages, having been encouraged by the late Arabella Churchill (Winston's granddaughter) who helped put Glastonbury on its feet both financially and organisationally.

Glastonbury's humungousness enables it to be divided up into all sorts of themed areas full of weird and wonderful sights, sounds and things to do. Lost Vagueness was the vaudevillian cabaret success that helped to promote the festival's wilder, edgier side throughout the late nineties. Now, a similar but wider variety of madcap entertainment is offered across three fantasy fields. Shangri-La – as the area is now known – (run by many of the former Lost Vagueness crew) smashes the boundaries of traditional festival fun with eclectic music, hot tubs, a Slumbarave (you get into pyjamas and frolic among the duvets), a scrumptious pizza diner, a Shackney music bar, kooky Club Dada cabaret and a freaky circus.

Trash City twists and distorts innocent imaginations with its Mutoid Waste alien-style installations: imagine a Tim Burton-style den of industrial art where vessels of grunting metal sculptures shoot flames all night. Here too is the NYC Downlow life-size street set built by

Block9. Guests buy moustaches to enter the dark dome where Horse Meat Disco DJs put on a storming 1987 disco complete with drag-queen catwalk shows.

In 2007 Michael's daughter Emily introduced The Park field, home to one of two onsite Silent Disco arenas. Emily first invited the Netherlands-based company in 2005 to overcome noise restrictions and they were so popular they've been on board ever since. People collect wireless headphones, and once inside, dance till dawn as DJs or live bands play music on two channels, creating a scene that looks every bit as amusing as it sounds. The Eavises and two others programme the Pyramid, Other, Jazz World and John Peel (new music) main stages. The music line-up never used to be announced to keep people guessing until just before the event, but in 2008, Barack Obama's favourite artist Jay-Z received an unprecedented media bashing when it was prematurely announced he was headlining.

What you can predict at Glastonbury is the emergence of a golden oldie on one of the main stages on Sunday afternoon (think Tony Bennett, Shirley Bassey), the biggest indie rock acts with albums to promote, a reunited band or two and a whole heap of quirky, alternative, jazztastic, folktastic, percussive, choral and gospel musicians in between.

WHEN Late June
GUIDE PRICE £175
CAPACITY 177,000
CAMPING Take your pick from the numerous camping fields encircling the festival arena. Due to the site's vastness, it's worth camping near to whichever stage or area you're likely to spend most of your time. Separate fields for camper vans and caravans are adjacent to the festival site. A designated family field, Cockmill Meadow, is conveniently near to the Kidz field and benefits from 24-hour campsite stewards and good lighting. The tent landslides of old should be avoided now that the festival has introduced new drainage systems.
TOP TIP Check that it's not a 'fallow' year (every five years or so they give the land a breather). If the festival is on, get there as soon as the gates open, otherwise you'll be lucky to find a decent pitch for your own tent, let alone for all the friends you want to camp with. And take comfortable footwear to cope with the miles of walking that's required from the car park to the campsite to the main stages all day, every day.
LIKE THAT, THEN YOU'LL LOVE France's largest green field festival, Festival des Vieilles Charrues (www.vieillescharrues.asso.fr) in the heart of Brittany, often bills similar headliners (and has better weather!).
LOCATION Worthy Farm, Pilton, Shepton Mallet, Somerset BA4 4BY

www.glastonburyfestivals.co.uk

GREEN MAN

Welsh weather is famous for its rainy days, pouring days and, well, just plain wet days. And it doesn't get much wetter than in the Brecon Beacons, even in August; but as scenery goes, it doesn't get much better than this either. You'd be hard pushed to find a more remarkable setting for a UK music festival, and a bit of drizzle doesn't dampen the spiritual connection that regulars have with this psychedelically titled Welsh event.

Since it began seven years ago, the Green Man has prospered. The number of genuine folk beards may have dwindled – today's audience isn't as hirsute as it once was – but the singer-songwriters on guitars and the indie-rock giants with their drums and bass just love performing to this crowd. The mostly Welsh, grown-up audience knows the difference between a Fender and a Les Paul, and relies on the programmers to book acts that won't attract the wrong 'towny' crowd.

The central point of the site is a natural amphitheatre, a flat vista that's watched over by Sugar Loaf Mountain in the far distance. Opposite the main stage are wide, gently sloping banks that rise up to more flat land. One side is lined with food stalls and cafés and on the other is a cobbled, gothic-walled garden. There, in the Stable Courtyard, is the Green Man

Café where acoustic sets by King Creosote and Lou Rhodes provided two of the most stirring musical moments at 2008's weekend.

The land this festival calls home belongs to Prince Charles' ex, Tiggy Legg Burke, whose family are by all accounts regarded as royalty in Wales. No other event takes place here, so the Green Man has done well to gain exclusive access since moving from Baskerville Hall, down the road. Sight lines don't get much better than at the main stage (thanks to those grassy banks) and the superb acoustics allow the subtlest of sonic movements to be heard.

Should the rain ever get too heavy, it wouldn't spoil the fun. Indie kids barely leave the Folky Dokey arena anyway, and with bands way down the bill in a class of their own (take Mumford and Sons as an example), who can blame them? Hedonistic the Green Man isn't, dance music is far from being the major draw here, although the Rumpus Room, programmed by Dominos Records, gets even busier after the main stage closes, playing electronic music until 5am.

Once the youngsters are asleep, dreaming of the puppets they crafted or the scientists that took their minds into space, it's time for those adults with green cards to relax. Well, in truth, they've probably done little more than stroll back and forth to the bar, but that doesn't mean they don't qualify for a massage in the Nature and Nurture rose-garden or an hour's pew inside the comedy tent.

Many, many years ago, Welsh locals would climb the Brecon hilltops and build fires to communicate with distant counties. Playing a pivotal role at the festival today, the new Campfire Field is the place to see out the twilight hours, discussing the Welsh poetry or Icelandic literature debate you caught earlier with new friends, as brave naked beings jump over the bonfire (this is, of course, neither

endorsed nor recommended). And as the flames die down, all paths lead to the Ends Up Bar, where night owls make the most of a 24-hour drinking licence.

The Green Man is an ancient mythological symbol believed to represent rebirth. So it's appropriate that the festival itself is undergoing some internal and structural changes, and some features of the site may be moved around. What remains a constant here is that rain never stops play – the Welsh are the heart and soul of this event and when has a drop of heaven's water ever kept them from having a good time?

WHEN Late August
GUIDE PRICE £105; kids under 11 are free, and campers and caravans are an extra £35 each.
CAPACITY Just seven years ago it was 300, but these days it's more in the region of 10,000.
CAMPING Flat fields have been split into separate areas for general camping, family camping and disabled

camping. You can also hire tents, tipis and caravans. Campfires and BBQs aren't permitted, but camping stoves or BBQs on legs are fine.
TOP TIP For just £30 more you can now pitch your tent the Monday before, giving you a whole week to explore the bubbling streams, rocky outcrops and endless rainbows of the Brecon Beacons, and enjoy clan bands.

LIKE THAT, THEN YOU'LL LOVE The End of the Road festival (p32) has a similar albeit more youth orientated music policy and because it doesn't take place until September, you've plenty of time to dust down your camping gear.
LOCATION Glanusk Park Estate, Crickhowell, Powys NP8 1LP

www.thegreenmanfestival.co.uk

CREW
&
ARTIST
PARKING

NO
ENTRY

Indietracks

You could say that Indietracks is where society's anoraks meet. It's a point further supported by the fact that the festival's 'controller' Stuart Mckay used to work at the Midland Railway Centre. While restoring trains by day and attending indiepop events in London by night, he hit upon this winning formula, combining both his passions in one event.

The steam-train journey from the Golden Valley campsite to the Midland Railway Centre is possibly the most romantic route to any festival there is. As you're chugging through the English countryside you'll begin to feel incredibly stylish when you notice the affected sartorial elegance of 'indiekids'. Turn a blind eye to the odd modern-day band T-shirt and you could be among the cast of a youth theatre production of *Murder On The Orient Express*.

Imaginative types should seek out the old-style first-class carriage where you can take a guess at what secret lives your fellow passengers may lead. Is that person sitting opposite... working as a spy...heading for a rendezvous with a clandestine lover...an escaped prisoner on the run from the law...or...modelling for a knitting pattern? Whoever they are, just remember to address them in your best clipped Queen's English tones should you wish to discuss the festival's programme.

Wander further along the train to the mail carriage and you'll discover the first festival band warming up, albeit with less instruments than you'll hear at their main stage set. The train's natural rhythm has a wonderful effect on their performance. If it's not an act you particularly want to see, just check the carriage bands' programme and hop on or off throughout the day to catch those that you do.

When you alight at the platform and the train chuffs away into the distance, head to the main stage in a large railway shed. Once you've obtained your wristband from the ticket conductor you can follow the train tracks towards the stage. It's in this high-topped corrugated shed that bands such as The Wedding Present and The Victorian English Gentlemens Club have headlined for the past few years, before Helen Love's late-night disco brings each night to a close.

Pay a visit to the stationary Victorian Buffet Cart on the way to the second stage, which is on the back of a truck. It's a good space, but not as good as the church; once used by rail workers, this relocated tin chapel looks very similar to the colonial buildings of New Zealand or South Africa. Inside you're likely to catch the navel-gazing eulogies from a fop in NHS glasses or hear confessional lyrics from shy young ladies who seem to be blissfully unaware of their own attractiveness.

On first impressions the Railway Centre site might look like a train cemetery, with quite a few static lines and sheds full of rolling stock. But even if the sight of a beautifully restored Series 55 Classic Deltic doesn't stoke your furnace, there are plenty of places to let off steam. There are the extremely niche pleasures of the National Forklift Museum and the enjoyable not-so-miniature railway to divert you. And if you're pissed off with pistons then

seek out something warm and furry, like the llamas, in the petting zoo.

You can buy food galore in Ripley (a short train ride away) but there is also a rather excellent transport café on the site, which serves simple 'caff' meals (think jacket potatoes, pasties and fry-ups) at a fraction of usual festival prices.

Indietracks isn't a party in a theme park or an attempt to create an atmosphere in a field, it offers genuine musical entertainment. Climb on board and enjoy the ride.

WHEN Late July
GUIDE PRICE £25 day ticket and £45 for the weekend.
CAPACITY 1,000
CAMPING The Golden Valley Camping & Caravan Park (www. goldenvalleycaravanpark.co.uk; about a mile from the festival site and reached via steam train) is in a woodland area of the Golden Valley hamlet alongside the Cromford Canal and, amazingly, it

has a jacuzzi (you can squeeze in up to eight people). Two adults and a tent costs £17.50 per night.
TOP TIP Take an open mind, you won't find big name bands here, this is a festival that celebrates the type of vibrant indiepop acts that Mckay believes deserve greater exposure. Still, if you're really pining to catch any of the church acts, chances are plenty of other people are too, so get

there early for a seat.
LIKE THAT, THEN YOU'LL LOVE Indiepops Christmas Twee is an early December all-dayer at the same site. All aboard (but do close the windows, it's a wee bit nippy, brrr).
LOCATION The Midland Railway Centre, Butterley Station, Butterley Hill, Ripley DE5 3QZ

It's very likely that many present-day festival fans you meet will have journeyed across the Solent several times in their youth, seeding their childhood discovery of caves, coves and castles into lifelong, happy memories. Throw in the fact that in many British families, there'll be someone who wistfully regrets not attending any of the original three Isle of Wight festivals in the late-'60s, and suddenly, catching the second wave of festival fever on the island makes all the sense in the world.

Over 100 million years ago, dinosaurs roamed the Isle of Wight. More than 40 years ago, thousands of hippies and mods bombarded the island for the rock festival. In 1970 (just three years after the first one), the number of festival attendees rose to 600,000, all eager to catch a glimpse of their American hero, Jimi Hendrix. The island's infrastructure couldn't cope with the unprecedented mayhem and the UK's first ever rock festival found itself as extinct as its Jurassic predeccesors.

It took the county council 32 years to allow Robert Plant to lead the charge in reviving the Isle of Wight festival as an annual affair. While the people behind the event may have changed, the atmosphere hasn't. There's undeniably a certain magic in the air at the main stage, one that you just don't always

experience at other festivals. Perhaps artists can sense the deep musical heritage and deliver their best sets. The Who, who performed at the 1969 event, put on an emotionally charged performance in 2004 (the same year that David Bowie sent the crowd bonkers with his Ziggy Stardust fireworks finale). R.E.M. united the 2005 crowd in a frenzied singalong and the likes of Coldplay and Muse could equally do no wrong in subsequent years.

Because it is first and foremost a music event, the majority of the Isle of Wight festival's budget is spent on great line-ups, which encourages regulars to snap up the early bird tickets within hours of them going on sale, without even knowing who's going to be on the bill. After the comeback successes of old hats such as The Doors and the Sex Pistols it seems that for many artists, playing at this prestigious event is an honour they're unlikely to turn down.

The recently introduced Big Top tent fits in 5,000 revellers and far from being a stage for B-list artists, you can expect to see just as many superstar acts here as over on the main stage. Smaller dance arenas cater for the beat nuts, giving ravers a chance to let off steam within short walking distance to the two main stages, so they can nip back over to hear a headlining act when their glow sticks have run out of juice. But this really isn't a rave fest, the bands are definitely the priority. And they are the type of bands regularly heard on radio playlists, there's not as many edgy, experimental new discoveries of the sort you'll find at Bestival (p22), for instance.

The Isle of Wight Council recently announced plans to transform the island into an eco island and, what's more, be entirely carbon neutral by 2020 (see Eco-friendly festivals, p139). The Isle of Wight Festival has followed the council's lead admirably, making a commitment to support long-term conservation projects, improve its operations and limit the environmental impact of the ticket-holders. Those '70s hippies would be proud!

WHEN Mid June
GUIDE PRICE £120 for non-camping tickets and £140 with camping.
CAPACITY 50,000
CAMPING We really admire that this is one of the only festivals that acknowledges that thieves exist and offers an online, step-by-step guide to protecting your belongings. Campers seeking some peace and quiet should head to the Sleepy Hollow camping area (don't worry, there aren't any headless horsemen here).
TOP TIP Walk your hangover off, why not, on the Tennyson Down, part of the island's 65-mile coastal path with stunning views of the Needles.
LIKE THAT, THEN YOU'LL LOVE A flotilla festival of boats! Cowes Week (www.cowesweek.co.uk) is the world's oldest regatta. Music, art and food make it one helluva street party on the island.
LOCATION Seaclose Park, Newport, Isle of Wight

HIPPY FAIRS

In the '60s some of the so-called hippies worked in offices and wore wigs and big Afghan coats at the weekends. By the '70s, us dedicated, true hippies had moved to the country and were embracing self-sufficiency. We were living the good life. Fairs allowed people who lived in quite isolated, remote areas to join various communities. The fairs in the '70s were often about connecting with the earth – there were Sun, Fire, Earth and Moon Fairs – we'd make flags and sculptures and I would perform rituals with my naked body decorated with mud. It was all very free spirited, with people playing music, drumming, smoking pot and dancing all night. The first one I remember was the Barsham Faire in the early '70s. It had a medieval theme and no electricity or vehicles were allowed on site. The Barsham Faires finished in 1976 but they inspired the Albion Fairs, which started a year or so later and become the most well known. Regular gatherings would move around East Anglia. We were tribes who were able to meet and communicate with similar people who lived just 60 miles away from us. Each event would use the same flagpoles, electric cables and water pipes. Similar do's took place in remote parts of Cornwall and North East Scotland and if we attended them then we'd all become brothers and sisters. At every fair we'd build dome structures together, finding the wood to construct the frames, spending two weeks building the site. Then there would be two magical days of the fair itself. Unplanned things would happen, beautiful relationships were formed and we just had to go with the flow.

BRUCE LACEY
81, PERFORMANCE ARTIST

Larmer Tree

Festivals, like so many things in life, are a matter of taste. Some people like theirs big and brash, where the idea of wading through hordes of excitable teenagers and dodgy geezers shouting 'Hash for cash!' feels like a good weekend away. Others, though, increasingly favour the 'boutique' festival format, where numbers are kept to a comfortable level (around the 5,000 mark), crime is virtually non-existent and the age ranges are as broad as the music policy.

Organisers of Larmer Tree, James Shepard and Julie Safe, skip to a business beat that other festival organisers sometimes ignore: the 'if it ain't broke, don't fix it' principle. Not once have they considered increasing their festival's capacity by moving to a larger site – they'd have had a problem with the name if they did – instead, they look for ways to get the best use out of their Dorset garden, a place they know as intimately as the resident peacocks do, having now staged their event here for 19 years and counting.

Situated in 11-acre gardens in the heart of Cranborne Chase, the land is an ancient royal hunting ground on the Dorset/Wiltshire border. Designed around 1880 by General Augustus Pitt Rivers as a pleasure garden for the estate workers, this location is perfect for a camping festival. Hidden halfway between Salisbury and the East Dorset market town of Blandford Forum, it's not the easiest of places to find and there aren't many signposts to help you, either. Just follow the brown heritage road signs through twisty, high-hedged hilly lanes until you land at the feet of the ticket inspectors at the entry gates.

The festival has built a loyal following; one couple love it so much they named their newborn son Larmer. Not that long ago, after seeing so many arrivals turn up early to watch Jools Holland and his big band play one Thursday, James and Julie decided to open their gates a day earlier, and now the festival begins on the Wednesday each year. Camping areas have since been widened and there's now a separate field for caravans and camper vans. One-day visitors benefit from their own parking field, and a larger car park on the other side accommodates those staying longer. There isn't much ground to cover between car boot and camping pitch, and extra provisions are made for disabled festival goers.

The main stage has a sloping lawn hugged by hedges and trees. Paths lead to random discoveries: alternative therapy spaces, open-mic stages and children's play areas. Kids have a great time here, at the adventure playground or donning their fancy dress to join the Sunday parade through the site (they can wear special wristbands you write your contact numbers on), or joining any of the other 150-plus activities. Teenagers get their own YouthZone area to keep them on a creative high, too. There's a Garden Stage for more live music and plenty of spots to sit and sup your tipple of choice. Food-wise, you can buy anything from Mexican nachos to West Indian gumbo and vegetarian pies, so there's never any danger of going hungry.

Musically speaking, the theme is heavily orientated in favour of world, folk and blues, although ska, reggae, rock and even dance music dives in at various points across the six venues. In short, there is enough of a repertoire to satisfy the bohemians as well as the more conservative types. Night owls happily carry on the party within the main site away from the camping areas, leaving the sleeping campers to enjoy their dreams in peace.

Larmer Tree's English country garden setting, great campsite views and boutique touches create an intimate festival that's difficult not to wax lyrical about.

WHEN Mid July
GUIDE PRICE Adult tickets range from £29 for a day to £177 for five days; youth (11–17) tickets start at £26 for a day and go up to £152 (five-day); and children (5–10) cost from £22 up to £124 (five-day). Under-5s go free.
CAPACITY 5,000
CAMPING Superbly organised with lovely countryside views. Within easy reach of the main festival site, the campsite offers facilities including disabled access, a camper van field and a one-night camping field (you have to leave by 11am).
TOP TIP If you want to party, Club Larmer within a corrugated-iron Victorian Tea Room hypnotises dancers with a mix of world music and contemporary club tunes until 3am. Elsewhere the Social tent is alive with insomniacs and happy hedonists.
LIKE THAT THEN YOU'LL LOVE Guilfest (www.guilfest.co.uk). It has loads of good family attractions and cranks the feel-good factor up a notch as the old-timer bands rouse an enthusiastic Guildford crowd. The crowd, though, is a lot 'townier' than at Larmer Tree.
LOCATION Larmer Tree Gardens, Donhead Saint Mary, Dorset SP5 5PY

www.larmertreefestival.co.uk

62

Bags of patience are required along the A roads that lead to this ridiculously popular festival – East Anglia has only one motorway and it's a busy old thoroughfare. But Latitude is worth risking those hours spent locked in a slow-moving convoy. Set in the private historical Henham Park Estate near Southwold, the location is mind blowing. Scattered with old oak trees, a winding lake and a magical forest so beautiful, this countryside helps to explain why all 20,000 tickets sell out faster than, well, the journey here.

Latitude has been sagely marketed at 20- to 40-somethings for whom knocking back warm, flat cider from a plastic bottle is but a hazy memory, one that's long been usurped by chilled pear cider poured over crushed ice. This refined class of mature, educated types (along with their junior family members) certainly don't want heavy metal, novelty jester hats and fast food. They want a Radio 4-friendly, full-on arts stimulation.

Entertainment tents are scattered over the compact site, pushing out various cutting-edge indie and pop bands, comedy, film, theatre and poetry in front of a peaceful lake. Across the water, over a well-trodden wooden footbridge, a narrow path leads up through towering pine trees to a serene clearing and the Sunrise Arena,

which is a great place to hear great leftfield, up-and-coming acts, such as Crystal Castles, Metronomy and Black Lips.

The aural offerings at Latitude vary from well-known headliners to lesser-known electro acts taking their first tentative steps on the inroads to the charts. The main Obelisk Stage – previously headlined by Franz Ferdinand, Sigur Rós and Interpol – is set on a gently inclining grassy field with a section of raised stadium-style seating at the back.

Famously, Latitude manages to attract the best comedy line-up outside of the Edinburgh Festival Fringe (p128); its pioneering move has since seen comedians, such as Ross Noble, Frankie Boyle and Phill Jupitus, turn into prime acts on the festival circuit. But be warned – if you don't want to be left outside the tent straining to catch the punch lines, you'll need to set off to the front a good hour or three before the headliners go on.

After the live music finishes at 11.30pm, you can party on until the wee hours at the Guilty Pleasures disco, where the fun cheesy pop tunes are enough to make your toes curdle. Anyone looking to up the tempo slightly can venture down to the woods to find a late-night sylvan rave going on.

Whenever your eardrums need a break, the popular poetry (featuring the likes of John Hegley, Keith Moore, Aisle16 and Attila The Stockbroker) and literary (past attending authors include Hanif Kureishi, Irvine Welsh, A. L. Kennedy and Dave Gorman) areas are furnished with plenty of beanbags and giant cushions to collapse on.

As you can imagine, with all these educated types roaming Latitude's grassy plains, the festival is pretty much absent of litter – numerous recycling and cigarette bins are well used. The bars require a deposit for your refillable plastic glass, encouraging you to return them (and if you don't, you can bet a few resourceful kids gladly will) and in turn there are fewer soggy cardboard cups strewn around the site. Probably, the only thing you're likely

to tread on will be a weekend supplement that's blown away in the breeze.

Wander across floating bridges to the camping areas and you're back at your tent within minutes of leaving the main arena. The fields here are lined with gourmet coffee vans, food tents, camping accessory shops, clean toilets and hot showers with queues that never seem to stretch that far.

Latitude may be a bit off the beaten track, but if you don't mind joining the hordes of adult, premium-beer-drinking festival goers – and can cope with the county's archaic road infrastructure – then relaxing in this gorgeous part of the world will more than provide the perfect antidote to the raucousness of your wild festival past.

WHEN Mid July
GUIDE PRICE £130 for a weekend camping ticket.
CAPACITY 25,000
CAMPING Clean, busy and close to the stages, the family camping tickets usually sell out far in advance. The others are divided into coloured zones; Yellow, Red and Green, each with their own toilets, water points and fire towers. A limited number of wheelbarrows are available to help shift gear from your car, and security people patrol the site so you'll feel safe.
TOP TIP Get comfy in front of the 'On The Lake' stage and watch the unravelling of beautiful dance performances. Previous choreographers include Sadler's Wells. And if you missed getting a ticket, just tune in to the various Radio 4 presenters who stream interviews and sessions live from the event.
LIKE THAT, THEN YOU'LL LOVE Should you be passing through the Netherlands in November the Crossing Border festival (www.crossingborder.nl) is considered to be one of the best literature events in the world, with artists such as Julian Cope and Rufus Wainwright.
LOCATION Henham Park Estate, Beccles, Suffolk NR34 8AN

www.latitudefestival.co.uk

Moor Music Festival

Perched right up in northern England, the Moor Music Festival has grown organically over the past few years. It is an esteemed family festival that doesn't require gallons of petrol to get to, and so has been rapturously extolled by locals who want an easy festival fix.

A main tent for live performances and two smaller ones patronising gentler acoustic strains or multimedia shows provide the lion's share of the entertainment. 2008 was blustery at times, but then everyone who heard the folk song 'On Ilkla Mooar Baht' at' ('on Ilkley Moor without a hat') will simply heed the lyrical advice and pack all-weather garb in future. Anyway, warmer summers are on the horizon, so hopefully the gear will remain in your backpack, unused.

The Earl Hickey Tribute Lounge was consumed by blues, jazz, world, folk and reggae; and the Green Room — a fully carpeted 1930s-style parlour with lots of big cushions, beanbags,

plants and artistic designs — resonated with animated conversation and activity all day. At night, the ravers joined the DJs in the main tent, leaving the Green Room in the hands of Leeds audio-visual specialists, Look & Listen, who billed Animat (among various artists) to rescore films with their own soundtracks. Organisers even threw in a few burlesque dancers for good measure, too.

Moor Music is non-profit-making and, in line with its non-corporate philosophy, food stalls serve only organic and fair-trade food. Families are well catered for — kids loved the camper van 'show and shine' competition, music workshops, being inventive with face paints and creating *papier mâché* masks.

It's doubtful this festival will ever be as colossal as the Somerset giant, although already its grass-roots atmosphere has led some to declare it a mini-Glastonbury for the North.

WHEN Early August
GUIDE PRICE £55 or £110 a family ticket (two adults and two under-12s); 13–16-year-olds are £5; 12s and under are free.
CAPACITY 2,500
CAMPING There are quiet, family and disabled camping areas.
TOP TIP Pack your swimmers and picnic on the spectacularly positioned lawns of Ikley's very own beautiful 1930s lido nearby.
LIKE THAT, THEN YOU'LL LOVE In early July Beat Herder (www.beatherder. co.uk) at Gisburn has stunning views of Ribble Valley and Pendle Hill and is twice the capacity. Beats are more frenetic and the music is boomed out of huge sound systems.
LOCATION In some grand Yorkshire countryside.

Summertime in London is alive with outdoor music all-dayers that cater for all ages and most musical bents. But – and for *Cool Camping* readers it's a big, gaping canvas hole of a 'but' – as brilliant as these can be, you can't camp at any of them.

Well, ok, the Hainault Forest Country Park isn't strictly in London, technically it's in Essex. But still, it lies within the M25 and the fact that you can catch a tube there makes it the closest camping festival to the English capital that you're likely to find.

Avant-garde sums up the musical direction of this youthful shindig. We say youthful, because generally it's the younger student-types who obsess over new bands. If the *NME* is tipping it, chances are Offset will be including it.

Any Greater London dweller willing to share their love of new wave, art rock and indie with their Essex neighbours (or anyone else wanting to make the most of the only night that campers are permitted in this forest) will have a great time here.

Over two days, two open-air stages and six marquees become the platforms for acts to blast out experimental, post-punk, folk, rock and so forth to a more than up-for-it audience. Managed by the people behind the now defunct annual TMF Rock Festival that used to hole up at the Orsett Showground (also in Essex), this festival has a wealth of experience behind it.

For 2009, Offset has improved its ticketing, bettered the quality of its sound systems and is continuing its support of underground club nights – last year Girlcore hosted the kitsch dance tent deploying switched-on promoters such as Durrr, Trailer Trash, Get Rude, Boombox and BuggedOut!. After all, even the youth need to stay on top of current trends.

WHEN Late August
GUIDE PRICE Weekend tickets are £45–55 with camping, and day tickets cost £28.
CAPACITY 5,000
CAMPING Campers are allowed onsite from 9.30am (the music starts at 12pm). This is the only time the forest is open to campers.
TOP TIP If you're not camping, the N8 night bus runs into central London via east London. Travel in numbers, you'll be glad of the company on the hour-long route back.

LIKE THAT, THEN YOU'LL LOVE Nearer to central London, Field Day (www.fielddayfestivals.com) is an alternative and leftfield, if slightly chaotic, non-camping weekender in early August.
LOCATION Hainault Forest Country Park, Redbridge, Essex IG7 4QN

READING

Some call it the Greatest Rock Festival in the World and it certainly is according to all those teenage boys who play air guitar in front of *Kerrang!* pin-ups in their bedrooms. These are the very music fanatics who race to Reading or Leeds each year to worship at the altar of rock, indie rock and metal.

During its almost 40-year-long reign, this monster weekender has proved that its audience is fussier than any other in the UK. When it comes to the billing, it seems Reading crowds don't like being fobbed off with anything they regard to be way off brief. Bands are 'bottled off stage' more regularly here than at any other event. Quite what Bonnie Tyler was ever doing on a Reading stage in 1988 is anyone's guess, but the fact that 50 Cent, My Chemical Romance and many other acts have been barraged with urine-filled plastic bottles or lager cans over the years has given this festival a fierce reputation.

However, by rigging boombastic sound systems, booking leading, heavyweight artists and pumping out enough beer to sink several battleships (or at least to render thousands of 20-somethings comatose by the night's end) more often than not it'll be a sea of rock handed salutes, not fists, that organisers see raised in appreciation most years.

The once Mean-Fiddler, now Festival-Republic-organised, double-whammy festival takes place in both Reading and Leeds during August's bank holiday weekend, featuring the same acts (just on different days). Reading fits in 10,000 extra ticket-holders, but Leeds is a prettier site, and the atmosphere is amazing at both.

Rock fans are pretty adept at punching the air, banging their heads and screaming at the top of their voices – usually all at once. Such is the quality of the line-up, though, that Reading also attracts plenty of London media and music industry blaggers. Even they leave their fashionably jaded views on music on the M4, buzzing around the backstage bar as excitably as the teenagers moshing in the main arena.

For the punters, getting in the thick of things (and that usually means squeezing inside 40,000-capacity arenas) is the only way to have a genuine Reading 'experience'. The universal dress code of rock's past – all pale denim and black leather – is no longer visible; today's crowd is less pedestrian in their dress sense but every bit as devoted to stadium rock as their predecessors were.

You're never far from the world's most esteemed rock gods and it's probably this very fact that turns initial ripples of excitement into body-surfing bedlam within seconds. We're talking about bands such as Metallica, Muse, Arctic Monkeys, Pearl Jam and the Kaiser Chiefs – so it's no wonder tickets continue to sell out in record time.

Over the years, household pop names have crept onto the main stages but there's also an Alternative Stage with spoken word, comedy (there's always been comedy, Eddie Izzard used to be a frequent guest in the early '90s), cabaret performers and film.

While the heart of this festival is rock, it does cater for dancers, too. The chemical beats of Underworld won over Reading's 1996 crowd; and after the emerging big beat stars Bentley Rhythm Ace blew the canvas roof off the tiny Dr Martens Stage in 1997, the club arenas grew bigger. Nowadays, Reading's third largest arena is dedicated to dance music and in 2008 the international act Pendulum finally had the chance to play, demonstrating the exact rock, post-rave mash up that Reading is all about.

WHEN Late August
GUIDE PRICE £155 for a weekend ticket. For an extra £10 you can enter the campsite from 6pm on Wednesday.
CAPACITY Reading 80,000; Leeds 70,000
CAMPING Usually the 'quiet' and 'family' camping areas are placed further away from the din of the main site. One of the campsites is situated near to a Silent Disco where you can

meet your friends and end the night. The campsites can feel feisty with all those teenage boys running amok, but the festival has an onsite 'police station' so there's a good level of security.
TOP TIP We come to rock! But for something completely different, head to ActionAid's dance and chill-out areas (pictured, right).
LIKE THAT, THEN YOU'LL LOVE June's Download festival (www.

downloadfestival.co.uk) takes place at Donnington Park, where the famous Monsters of Rock festivals of old used to attract the true 'mettlers' in their droves. Smaller in size (with just three stages) Download boasts a similar big band line-up.
LOCATION Richfield Avenue, Reading, Berkshire RG1 8EQ

www.readingfestival.com

School-age children in the 1980s lived for taping the Top 40 off the radio, then scribbling down and memorising the lyrics. It was the only way to spend Sunday evenings. Then there was *Top of the Pops*, which propelled a world of big hair and new-romantic glamour out of portable TVs and into their monochrome bedrooms.

A baby on the festival circuit, Retrofest has been pretending that the past 20 years never happened. Teenage kicks are relived with gusto as reformed '80s chart toppers such as Kajagoogoo, 10CC and Boney M churn out their catalogue of hits. Really it's the combination of all the acts that makes this festival the ultimate retro experience. It can turn into quite a boozy affair, but that's a good thing – nostalgic singalongs sound even better after a few drinks.

Many once-famous bands have already graced this four-year-old event, but Retrofest should continue to be a flashback – not flash-in-the-pan – success. Seeing as it only takes place once a year (although there are plans to take the brand abroad) there are plenty of eighties one-hit-wonders to keep the line-up fresh.

A Club Tropicana Beach with a cocktail bar, a glitterball disco and a headphone 'silent' disco are ideal spots for practising formation dancing. Afterwards, head to the Retro Ritz Cinema (via the retro sweetshop) and settle down in front of one of the era's celluloid classics.

Leg warmers and sweatbands on? Let's get physical, physical, among a brazenly up-for-it crowd eager to relive favourite '80s music memories. Ok, so you never did cop off with Andrew Ridgeley or Kim Wilde, and with hindsight, electric blue mascara wasn't such a good look after all. But the bands were more fun to watch than any decade since.

WHEN Late August
GUIDE PRICE Adult day/weekend/with camping tickets cost £40/£64/£76. The same deal for children comes in at £20/£32/£38.
CAPACITY 10,000
CAMPING You have to buy 'tent' tickets, which are checked at the gates as you pass in and out. The camping

areas are doubling in size for 2009 with improved facilities and safety-guarding CCTV cameras.
TOP TIP Pack lozenges and honey for hot drinks at the campsite, as you'll be singing till you're hoarse.
LIKE THAT, THEN YOU'LL LOVE When you can't see the real thing, tribute bands are the next best option.

Glastonbudget (www.glastonbudget.co.uk) is the biggest tribute band festival in Europe and bills acts such as Oasish, Guns 2 Roses, Beat That and The Jamm in Leicestershire every May.
LOCATION Strathclyde Country Park, 366 Hamilton Road, Motherwell, Lanarkshire ML1 3ED

www.retrofest.co.uk

CLASS OF '88

We set out early on Saturday morning and hoped to arrive at Glastonbury by afternoon. It felt similar to setting off for a rave in the countryside somewhere. In fact that's exactly what it was in some ways. Mainstream pop concert promoters began to recognise the potential of staging dance-orientated production shows to attract this now commercial crowd. Glastonbury was the first organisation that allowed party promoters to hire their own marquees onsite. We'd dropped the compulsory travel pill and happily bopped our heads to Fabio & Grooverider mix-tapes for the journey's duration. Almost everyone we knew involved with rave culture planned to attend and party for days. This year the bill included the Happy Mondays and World Dance. We bumped into the rave crowd as soon as we got there, then Sinead O'Connor hit the stage with 'Nothing Compares 2 U' (a favourite for both Keith and me, it reminded us of our ex-girlfriends). Although she appeared smaller than a tin-soldier her voice was as loud as a hurricane. Plagued with repressed emotion we both started crying, doubt and regret running through our minds. Were we really that bad? Further down the hill a daisy chained group of girls were interweaving tents singing loudly. We raced down to join the human train and soon our chain reached the outer boundaries of the field stretching across a vast region of synthetic based habitats. Hundreds, possibly thousands sang the chorus line waltzing the field. If our lives ended then and there, our tombstones would bear the inscription Been There Seen It Done It.

WAYNE ANTHONY
AUTHOR, FILM-MAKER

Edited extract from Wayne Anthony's *Class of 88: The True Acid House Experience* (Virgin Books)

'Welcome to Sham Air, boarding is in five minutes, put your bags on the carousels and walk through.' A tray of arrival drinks is thrust under noses, a fake scanner zaps bodies and without further ado, you're in. The faux airline cabin looks convincing and makes for an intriguing (and possibly the smoothest ever) entry to a festival. This is the non-commercial, creatively bursting world that is Shambala – alive with random fun and games for all ages.

Shambala is a prime example that initial impressions don't always count. At first glance this event resembles a rural village fête, not a celebrated, quirky festival. But then again, it's only Friday, not everyone has arrived yet, and the music hasn't even started. The gentle introduction is perfect for easing in to the weekend. There's no rush, so why not take a relaxing pew in the Pub Garden, brew in hand, before heading off in search of festival frolics?

There are kids' activities everywhere; while creative workshops provide splashes of colour and bursts of energy to the place; and the air is thick with the smell of delicious foods. When the sun goes down and the cover of darkness creeps over the site, there's a shift away from the fête vibe as the atmosphere steps up a gear and the revelry begins. A gentle thud of reggae and dub beckons a sea of white dreads

onto dancefloors, lights begin to twinkle across the lake and the adventures begin.

Shambala has been going for 10 years and has developed, until recently, purely through word of mouth. There's a strong West Country meets Midlands following. Originating just outside Bristol before moving to Northamptonshire in 2007, the dedicated regulars are more than willing to put in the extra miles to head north.

Every footstep opens a new world of escapism. Stalls and smaller tents are arranged in a central huddle and walking around them you pass the main bar, two music stages, the entrance to the woods, the lake (lined with hot tubs) an acoustic stage, workshops, and before you know it you're back at the kids' area. This meander elicits conversations with all sorts – woodcarvers, hoopla dancers, two huge pantomime reindeer and a group of boys building a time capsule covered in silver foil.

A magical path lit by inflatable sculptures leads through the trees and into the thick of the woods where you'll find large climbing nets tangled with kids of all ages. Continuing the Shambala discovery tour, you'll happen upon the large Wishing Tree to pin all your secret hopes on. In the Geisha Lounge you can marvel at the attempts of brave warblers who are guaranteed a hearty round of applause from the amiable audience, regardless of their karaoke talents. The geisha girls look amazing and act every inch the hospitable hostesses, their painted faces of innocence belying their spanking booth (it's surprising how popular a pay-for spanking actually is).

As time slips by over this colourful weekend, chaos ensues, infecting everyone, slowly, cautiously, until by Saturday everyone's well and truly submerged in loonesville.

Musically, Saturday kicks off on the main stages with frantic hysteria as musicians such as the gypsy group Destroyers and the Punjabi Dhol Blaster drummers get people moving. Over in the amazing Kamikazi Kabaret tent, stunning trapeze acts are met with rapturous applause. An array of fancy dress costumes parade the site. Everything becomes a blur. What happens at Shambala, stays at Shambala. We can't wait for next year.

WHEN Late August
GUIDE PRICE Adults cost £99 each. Teens (15–17) are £59; children over five are £25 each and car fees are charged on top.
CAPACITY 29,000
CAMPING The fields are near the car park, so popping back to remember a forgotten pair of wellies or extra jumper, should you need either, only takes minutes. It's a refreshingly non-claustrophobic atmosphere. You can hire ready-to-move-into yurts and tipis if you'd rather not tent it. Wood for campfires is provided.
TOP TIP Grab a shower before the morning rush else you'll be queuing for an hour.
LIKE THAT, THEN YOU'LL LOVE More pipe smoking, wheelbarrow racing and medieval sporting fun can be had in Cumbria at the Egremont Crab Fair (www.egremontcrabfair.org.uk) in September.
LOCATION Secret location in Northamptonshire (revealed only once you've got your ticket!)

www.shambalafestival.org

SUNRISE CELEBRATION

Sunrise Celebration is an unashamedly hippy festival. In fact, it's been so relaxed that over the years it hasn't always kept its beaded head above water (financially as well as geographically). 2008 was such a washout that the May event was called off. Despite the rain and the odd monetary hiccup, organisers seem to return each year with a new event.

At the festival's heart lies the Sacred Hearth – a space for shrines, temples and shamanic dancing. A wooden circle, aptly named Woodhenge, is aligned to Glastonbury Tor; and the festival's mantra quotes Gandhi: 'Be the change that you want to see in the world'.

'Sustainability' is not just a greenwashing catchphrase at Sunrise. Stages are solar powered, equipment is moved around the site by horse and cart, and urinals are straw bales. The festival preaches what it practises too, with a Green Innovations area devoted to workshops with talks on renewable energy. On top of these carbon-footprint-shrinking lessons are 13 arenas, healing fields and heaps of dreadlock-friendly dub, trance and ambient flavoured music. You won't find any Glastonbury headliners playing, but there may be a couple of familiar acts (such as the Orb and Dub Pistols). Still, this isn't a weekend for fine-tuned timetables. Instead, you'll chance upon interesting smaller performances in venues like the late-night hangout, the Bimble Inn, which has grown from a single tent into an entire area with bars, stages and a dressing-up tent.

Everyone – whether a former traveller, a Glastonbury old-timer or the most non-environmentally aware consumer – will have a great time here and may even feel inspired to help make the world a better place.

WHEN Late May
GUIDE PRICE £120 per adult, a family is £200. Teen tickets (16–18-year-olds) cost £65 and children (5–15-year-olds) are £25.
CAPACITY 10,000
CAMPING An 'alternative camping' area of tipis and yurts has its own clean compost toilets, secure fencing and shower and sauna facilities. There is a horse and cart service running from the car parks to luxury camping areas. Spiral Sun Solar Showers in the campsite insist on the use of biodegradable soap only.
TOP TIP Take an open mind, a love of learning and a tip for the horse and cart should you need a hand with your camping gear.
LIKE THAT, THEN YOU'LL LOVE The Big Green Gathering (www.big-green-gathering.com), the original non-profit-making, hippy, eco-conscious festival, is back in business.
LOCATION An organic farm in south Somerset (above sea level!).

www.sunrisecelebration.com

 **IN THE PARK**

Over hills and glens they come – T in the Parkers by the thousand – swinging sacks of provisions, lugging rigging for shelter and swigging flagons of eye-watering brews. Many wear tribal colours, in support of an ancient (football) team or merry (rock) band; others dress up as pirates or, more bizarrely, as items of fruit. And some wear very little at all – regardless of the weather – except for a splash of blue paint on their faces, like ancient warrior Picts – they come here not to do merciless battle but smiley, ravin' partyin'.

If Mel Gibson ever fancied making *Braveheart: The Musical* (with guitarists' 'axes' replacing battleaxes), for research purposes he need look no further than T in the Park. Scotland's long-running rock festival is a good-natured jamboree of gigging, singing, dancing, fancy dress and Celtic-flavoured carousing.

How awesome is this atmosphere? Well, the parties start in the campsite, and some patrons, laden down with supplies, head straight there, set themselves up and stay put for the entire weekend. Sure, some of the world's biggest and best bands are playing across 12 stages in the main arena, but the self-contained campsite offers fairground attractions, food vans, shops and (should you be so inclined) one huge round-the-clock knees-up.

T in the Park is renowned across the UK's summer cultural landscape as one of the most giddily celebratory festivals on the calendar. The performers, dazzled by the passion of the fans and the mellow sophistication of the backstage facilities, frequently cite it as the greatest stop on their international touring schedules. The Killers class their 2007 headline slot (which came two weeks after their ill-fated Glastonbury appearance) as one of their greatest-ever shows. Radiohead, who delivered a legendary set back in '95, were totally 'bummed' that they couldn't fit in a return visit in 2008. And as for Scottish bands...Let's just say that the reception from the home crowd, whether for The Proclaimers (T's patron saints), Biffy Clyro (T's most prolific performers) or KT Tunstall (T's home-grown star, raised in nearby Fife), is always deafeningly rapturous.

Scotland's original and best music festival is sponsored by Tennants brewers (hence the 'T'), and has been since its inception in 1994. Over the years T's undergone several changes. The original site was a compact, fairly bog-standard park near Glasgow, but in 2005 it moved to the much-expanded venue of an old airfield situated in rolling Perthshire farmland. These days the 'early bird' advance ticket allocation sells out a full year in advance, while remaining tickets get snapped up long before the event.

Facilities have improved too. Security and policing is thorough and fair. Traffic flow and parking have been improved and in 2006 organisers introduced a Healthy T area, full of gourmet gastro-nosh. So although many punters will still spend the entire 72 hours subsisting on lager'n'chips, many others will be wolfing down buffalo burgers, locally sourced seafood and risotto.

But like any festival worth its weight in gold, T in the Park is mostly about the music. Catch the stars of tomorrow in the T Break tent, enjoy some folk'n'roll in the Ceilidh tent, go clubbin' in the Slam tent (hosted by the legendary Glasgow club of the same name) and wave a big flag in the air like you just don't care in front of the main stage...All in the highly convivial – if occasionally over-lubricated – atmosphere.

Most of all, T in the Park, as *Braveheart*'s medieval hero would yell, offers its guests... FREEDOM!...to rock.

WHEN Early to mid July
GUIDE PRICE From £85 for a day ticket to £195 for weekend camping tickets; car parking is £15.
CAPACITY 85,000
CAMPING The atmosphere in the campsites is legendary and hundreds of festival goers stay put there for the entire weekend. They house a cinema, a Silent Disco, the Duracell Powerhouse Club, Cabaret Voltaire's Boom Bus, a popular fairground, food stalls, bars and lockers. The Residence is a luxury camping option combining yurt and tipis for hire with access to the hospitality area.
TOP TIP Fancy Dress Friday was a recent and now regular addition – so don't forget your feather boas and vintage hats.
LIKE THAT, THEN YOU'LL LOVE T in the Park shares artists with Oxegen (www.oxegen.ie) in Kildare, Ireland on the same weekend, which is equally boozy and boisterous.
LOCATION The Old Air Field, Balado, Kinross-shire KY13 7NW

In the beginning there was the rock festival: bad food, warm lager, shouty rock, lots of mud and no washing for days. Next up was rave: repetitive beats, overstimulated crowds, megawatt sound systems and trouble with the police. Then, in the mid nineties, The Big Chill took its 'back room of a club' concept to the great outdoors and began changing the face of music festivals forever.

From their small events in the Black Mountains (1994) and Larmer Tree Gardens (1996–2001), where guests once parked their cars next to their tents, via Lulworth Castle (2002) to its present, gorgeous Herefordshire home at Eastnor Castle's Deer Park, The Big Chill created a blueprint that spawned the many 'boutique' events that now fill the summer calendar.

Marching several steps ahead of the initial chill-out music wave, the first Big Chills were adored for their then-pioneering concept. Eclectic music programming combined WOMAD-friendly music with leftfield London club nights and threw in everything from electronic dance music to classical via jazz, hip-hop, blues, folk, reggae and world music, all of which you could hear in one of Mr Scruff's DJ sets alone.

The period when chill-out compilations saturated the pop charts coincided with The Big Chill's move from the Larmer Tree site to Eastnor Castle, and having always been an ambient, horizontal orgy of sounds, the public's sway in favour of the rockier electronic music that was emerging meant the festival had to work harder to lure an increased capacity.

By 2008 the megastar Leonard Cohen, comedian Bill Bailey and comedy men-of-the-moment The Mighty Boosh brought the festival to the attention of a mainstream audience. To pacify the original 'Chillers', Little Dragon, Ninja Tune's Flying Lotus, the rabble-rousing Disco Shed and the terraced Rizla Arena's Invisible Players DJs, supplied just a few of the magical highlights.

Two big outdoor stages, a club tent and various DJ bars are scattered within easy walking distance of each other; and a Comedy tent programmed with various bigshots on their way to the Edinburgh Festival Fringe (p128) mixes up the entertainment. The main stages finish at 2am, when anyone still going can converge outside the 24-hour Big Chill Radio cabin to dance to guest DJs, albeit at low volume.

The Ombudsman and Amukidi VJs beam cutting-edge visuals from all stages and the Media Mix tent, which used to be a huge cinema and a performance space, is now a music stage, too, depending on what time you turn up (it stays open until 5am).

Comfort is one of The Big Chill's greatest selling points. From the high-quality food to the professionally mixed cocktails, via the original Body & Soul holistic haven, the hot showers and endless rows of rigorously cleaned (award-winning) loos, you'll barely notice you're sharing facilities with 34,999 other people. Sloping, well-tended lawns are dotted with art installations and ancient trees, and at night the lights hover around the site like a warming, safeguarding halo.

By the very nature of this relaxed party, many Big Chillers now come with their offspring – although you will probably see more toddlers than teenagers. The family field is perfectly situated near the main arena and the kids' entertainment tents include a Club Mum disco, swings and puppet shows.

So, there you have it. A comfortable, friendly camping weekend where you can chance upon unknown bands and now, some bigger names, too. Other festivals may have since improved on The Big Chill's blueprint, and some revellers prefer a different musical barrel altogether, nonetheless the festival is a super-sociable get-together in a beautiful and (usually) sunny part of the world.

WHEN Early August
GUIDE PRICE £120 for adults and under-12s go free.
CAPACITY 35,000
CAMPING North camping is generally noisy and Quiet Camping isn't so quiet any more either. The views as you walk to the site are incredible, the main arena glimmers like a jewel from the moment the lights are switched on on Thursday evening. New in 2009, The Lost Hotel rents yurt accommodation and has a spa and café.
TOP TIP Check the Forum for tips, posters chat on there all day long. Arrive as soon as the gates open, you won't want to be in Friday rush-hour traffic when you can be here soaking in every beautiful moment. Beat the queues for the ridiculously popular Pieminister stall, have a pie for breakfast! We recommend the Mr Porky Pie, Moo Pie, Heidi Pie, and well, most of them really...
LIKE THAT, THEN YOU'LL LOVE Now you've warmed up, head straight on to Bloom (www.bloomfestival.com), which takes place the next weekend. It's less than 30 miles away and boasts a fantastic dance music line-up among its many other attributes.
LOCATION Eastnor Castle, Ledbury, Herefordshire HR8 1RL

www.bigchill.net

EASTNOR
DEER PARK

RULES FOR FISHING

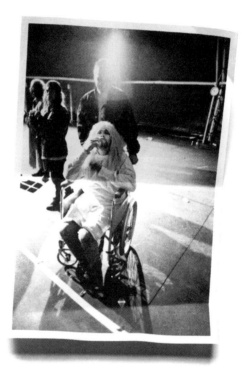

NIRVANA'S LAST UK GIG

Reading 1992 and Nirvana showed up late: maybe they'd just flown in from another festival in Europe. I can't recall. Kurt came over and made sure I had enough to drink. Someone was shouting something about a wheelchair. "They're going to wheel me on stage in that," Kurt explained. "It's like a joke on all the people who've been having a go at us, saying that I'm in hospital, OD'd." It was almost time to go on stage: someone dimly asked someone else whether Kurt should wheel himself on stage or… "Hey!" I shouted, pissed off my head. "Let me push that! I can push that! Let me push Kurt on to the stage. It'd be way funnier." No one could think of a good enough excuse to stop me. I have little memory of what happened next. There was a drunken wheelchair chase where I pushed Kurt round in ever-increasing circles in hot pursuit of the L7 girls on the side of the stage. Neither of us knew where the stage's edge was: we could easily have gone over. The lights. That's all I can remember. The lights. You can't see a single face. The crowd is invisible, and all that you feel is this incredible euphoric roar that increases every step you make towards the microphone. "He'll be OK," Krist Novoselic [Nirvana's bassist] reassured the crowd, pointing out to the wings, where we slowly materialised: "With the help of his friends and his family, he'll survive."

EVERETT TRUE
JOURNALIST, AUTHOR & EDITOR

Edited extract from *Nirvana: The True Story* by Everett True (Omnibus Books)

Swirly flags circle the breeze. Face-painted beauties on stilts whirl around the trees. New-agers, travellers, dreads, trustafarians and fresh-faced students merge as one beating tribe.

All around, people are piling into rave tents to dance under illuminated constellations. Glow sticks are old hat, instead, girls are sporting glow-in-the-dark underwear and above them neon lights shimmer from branches. Wrongly dismissed as a psy-trance rave, Glade Festival increasingly embraces more music genres and entertainment now runs late into the night.

The organisers have even moved site for 2009, fearing a repeat of 2007's rainfest, which transformed the Glade's previous Berkshire home into the kind of quagmire only hippopotamuses could enjoy. These days, the natural amphitheatre of Hampshire's Matterley Bowl forms the setting for this evolving festival.

Ever since its conception as Glastonbury's first dance arena, the Glade's signature sounds have been psychedelic, experimental electronica and Detroit techno (Eat Static and Squarepusher). Further onsite spaces advocate different kinds of dance music including breaks, deep house and trance, so all preferences are catered for.

Aware that attendees' tastes have matured with each passing year, organisers have created more intimate, boutique spaces to excite their regulars; and Mutoid Waste-style installations litter the site.

The Glade may be growing bigger, but it'll never be too grown-up. Hardy old-timers and newcomers alike will relish the fringe madness: getting hitched in the marriage parlour before burrowing down a Rabbit Hole warren to be fed fruit by a Cheshire Cat. It all makes perfect sense at the time.

WHEN Late July
GUIDE PRICE Adults £125, students £99 and camper van tickets £45.
CAPACITY 10,000
CAMPING As well as camping fields, there are 60 bell tents (www.belltent.co.uk), each sleeping six to eight people, available for rent at about £400

for the weekend. For that you get a morning paper delivery service, hot tubs and even a bedouin café.
TOP TIP You can now invite your friends who aren't into psy-trance. The festival is turning into lots of little festivals, with different areas dedicated to a variety of music styles, including

a live music stage.
LIKE THAT, THEN YOU'LL LOVE For bigger doses of trance, head to the huge GlobalGathering (www.globalgathering.co.uk), near Stratford.
LOCATION The Matterley Bowl, Matterley Estate, Winchester, Hampshire SO24 0HY

www.gladefestival.com

Festival organisers who've partied hard throughout their youth obviously find the process of selling tickets much less stressful than their competitors. From the off, several hundred loyal friends will be waiting in the wings raring to support the event wholeheartedly. And because like attracts like, if the crowd is a social one, the parties will be lively and word will soon spread. It doesn't take long for our island's professional hedonists to sniff out the latest hot ticket, and this one is so hot, it literally sets dancefloors on fire.

The Secret Garden Party isn't a music festival per se, although the 'head gardener', festival boss Freddie Fellowes, has really grown into his role, bettering the line-up with every passing year. The festival has also worked on improving the sound quality over time. In 2008 Grace Jones, Zero 7 and Lykke Li put the systems through their paces and the non-mainstream acts (ranging from gypsy to ska) on the bill sounded just as good.

Everything takes place on Freddie's family's land, a lake and garden that his grandfather sculptured with a government grant back in 1977. A main bar affords the best views of the principal 'Great' stage at the bottom of the hill. There are two more outdoor rigs – the Where the Wild Things Are stage and a theatre and music space – and eight covered arenas run by external promoters (spots are allocated to those that send in the nuttiest creative proposals).

There is so much artistic input that all your senses are overloaded. Life in this temporary Cambridgeshire encampment succeeds because of the interaction of the attendees. From the popular treasure hunt, where guests are aided or thwarted by sorcerers, wizards and zombies, to the theatre company that uses members of the audience as props – these are the moments everybody remembers, long after tents have been packed away.

A four-day party that appeals to 8,000 seasoned revellers requires a lot of variety, and this is where the festival wins heaps of gold stars. Among the twilight maypole dancing, the charades, the Storytelling Shed and chocolate parlours there is plenty to keep the kids active, too – just leave them designing pizza, making masks or bopping at the disco any time you need to fall into the hands of a healing practitioner in the Sanctuary field. There's dancing for the adults too, of course – 2009 features a two-storey, 40-capacity floating dance pontoon called the Tower of Babel (accessible only by boat), but just make sure you've checked it out before it is blown up in a pyrotechnic spectacular on the Saturday night.

The Action Camps provide a utopia of play spaces where madness erupts and kindred souls run wild. There are structures to climb on, hay bales to throw, costumes to squeeze into, historical personas to adopt, conspiracies to spread, doctors and nurses to get entangled with...So be sure to pack playful imaginations alongside your fancy millinery.

2008's highlight was the setting alight of a galleon boat dance space – the flames cut through by fireworks. An Avant Garden exhibited installations and multi-media works by various artists, and Camp Vegas impressed with roulette wheels and strip poker. The *Idler* magazine encouraged poets, philosophers and writers to ponder over the big philosophical issue: 'how to live'. In 2009, Explorer Camp takes the debating baton, featuring real-life travel explorers; and Science Camp will be back, bigger than ever.

Word about this rather splendid weekend is now well and truly out. Expect it to be the hottest ticket for some years to come.

WHEN Late July
GUIDE PRICE £137 per adult; 14–17 year olds (have to be accompanied by an adult) are £110; children aged 13 and under are free; camper van tickets cost £40.
CAPACITY 8,000
CAMPING There's normal, everyday camping, and then (if you feel like splashing out) in a field surrounded by hedges, there's Boutique Camping, with yurts, tipis, podpads, private showers, posh toilets and communal yurts (for loungin in) under the branches of old oak trees.
TOP TIP Get there now, before the numpties do.
LIKE THAT, THEN YOU'LL LOVE Blissfields' (www.blissfields.co.uk) 1,000-capacity festival is smaller, and not as mad, but the prices are low – a weekend ticket is £44.95 and for that you get to enjoy tents bursting with various entertainment, nestled away in Hampshire woodland. Blissfields will celebrate its 10th anniversary in July 2010.
LOCATION Abbots Ripton, Huntington, Cambridgeshire PE28 2PH

www.secretgardenparty.com

Fed up of paying an arm and a leg, only to battle through crowds and end up nowhere near the front, straining to see the headliners? Do you stay at home and watch the same performances loop on TV? Yes maybe, but you'll miss all the fringe frissons. Organise your own boutique affair? Six friends united by a love of rock music did just that and came up trumps.

Unlike the colossal corporate music events, this micro-site is so user-friendly that you don't need ordnance instructions to find your way around. Punters can walk several rings around the field in a matter of minutes. The site's low maintenance means the entry fee is low, too.

You'll find a fantastic mixture of British, mostly guitar-led bands on the main stage (past guests have included Frank Turner, Art Brut, InMe, The King Blues and The Duke Spirit); various DJs enticing crowds into the GreenHouse shed and eclectic fusions of folk, rock, pop, indie and metal ringing out of the Leaf Lounge.

Tasty food is fresh and locally sourced. The bar, manned by the organisers' better halves, is stocked with local ales and Badger's Bottom cider (brewed at Hayles Fruit Farm, just down the road). Do remember to check the website for Friday's fancy dress theme, but expect the unexpected – previous years have included 'dead people' and 'countries of the world'.

To book the best up-and-coming bands, DJs and comedians possible, without clashing with other festivals, the organisers now run the festival over the third weekend in July. The only rules are that everyone has to help keep the place spotless, and be off site by Sunday afternoon.

If you're craving underground sounds in a beautiful setting, miss this at your peril!

WHEN Mid July
GUIDE PRICE Weekend tickets are approximately £47 and kids under-10 are free. It's also possible to get day tickets – see website for details.
CAPACITY 2,500
CAMPING The camping area has stunning views. There weren't any showers at the first two festivals (so mud-sliding isn't recommended), but they do have fresh spring drinking-water posts. On the bright side the fields are spacious so you won't end up too close to your neighbours.
TOP TIP Don't leave without a souvenir, Cider Smiles compilation CDs, sold onsite, feature many of the artists you'll have heard over the weekend.

LIKE THAT, THEN YOU'LL LOVE
The Peak District's Y-Not Festival (www.ynotfestivals.co.uk), on the last weekend of July, is the closest to this in terms of music and atmosphere. In fact, the two festivals offer a deal if you buy tickets for both events.
LOCATION Upcote Farm, Withington, Cheltenham, Gloucestershire GL54 4BL

www.twothousandtreesfestival.co.uk

Truck Festival is a tiny, fiercely independent and real alternative gem on the British music festival calendar; an event that's grown by word-of-mouth and become truly cult. Confusingly, the title doesn't derive from the first music stage they used, which consisted of one solitary truck and trailer, but after a compilation CD picked up by one of the organisers.

Now held on a small livestock farm (yes you will be dancing next to tractors) in a leafy, rural village in Oxfordshire, organisers still use a truck for the main Truck Stage. They have slowly added several more areas, including a cowshed barn (used as a manure store during the rest of the year), a geodesic dome specialising in electronica and hip-hop, a Village Pub Rock Stage and a comedy tent called The Pavilion. Handmade wooden signs and decorations brighten the site, and at night, five huge searchlights pierce the sky.

Although famous bands like the Magic Numbers, Foals and Maxïmo Park; and international names such as the Lemonheads, John Otway, Josh T Pearson and alternative-country outfit Lincoln have all strummed their way through a decade of Truck, most of the music here comes courtesy of local, and often relatively unknown musicians longing for their big break (see Festivals for New Music, p158).

Founder Robin Bennett and his brother Joe developed the festival from a grass-roots level. Returning from a British music festival feeling disappointed one year, they set out to create a downscaled version closer to home. Local bands were booked for the first one-day event, which attracted 1,000 guests. The popularity of Truck grew and, despite a washout year in 2007 when most of Oxfordshire was submerged in freak floods, everything has been going, and growing, pretty smoothly.

Team Truck has thus far resisted calls to make the festival larger, preferring to maintain an intimate experience for the 5,000 people lucky enough to get tickets. Untainted by any corporate sponsorship and conducted with plenty of tongue-in-cheek country humour, the festival attracts quite a spectrum of fans – local kids going to their first festival, new-music lovers in search of fresh bands and old-timers who have been every single year since 1998. For teens who choose Truck as their first festival experience before attempting giants such as Reading or Glastonbury (and Robin knows this market well, he was 19 when he created Truck) parents can feel happy that the organisation prides itself on being safe.

The two-day gala relies on local assistance. The neighbouring farm owner makes burgers onsite, the parish vicar sells ice cream to fundraise for local causes and other treats are sold by the local Didcot Rotary Club; so you're never short of decent, just-cooked fare to feast on. Like the drinks, the food is cheaper than at other festivals, and all profits go to charity.

Truck indulges in its fair share of hedonism too, which you'll soon discover if you find yourself in the cowshed at 2am watching the crazed techno of Altern-8. In fact, come 9pm on Saturday all the stages switch to dance music, which cleverly creates groupings of energetic parties all over the site for people to delve in and out of as much or as little as they please.

The campsite is in an adjoining field and although summer weather in Oxfordshire is generally glorious, do bring wellies (it is a farm after all) as well as waterproof clothing, just in case. The overall spirit is very much about mucking in for laid-back and cheery rural fun. In short, Truck Festival is the perfect bite-sized, outdoor festival experience for anyone who fancies ditching the city for a weekend and escaping to the English countryside.

WHEN Late July
GUIDE PRICE £60–75
CAPACITY 5,000
CAMPING Camping is in a scenic field surrounded by farmland and trees. Showers are limited but most people arrive on Saturday morning and stay one night, so are happy to make do with their own cleaning wipes.
TOP TIP Arrive hungry; the non-profit-making Rotary Club sells burgers, pasta, salads, Indian food, doughnuts, veggie burgers and banana smoothies. Then for a change of scene, the breakfasts and Sunday roasts served in the village pubs are also scrumptious and not to be missed.
LIKE THAT, THEN YOU'LL LOVE The Bennett family's newest event, the three-day environmentally conscious WOOD festival (details can be found at www.thisistruck.com) has a solar-powered stage made of (you guessed it) wood, all the food and showers are heated by wood-burning stoves and most people arrive by bicycle.
LOCATION Hill Farm, Church Road, Steventon, Oxon OX13 6SW

V festival

Consumers buy albums, artists shift millions of CDs; in turn they become richer and more in demand, and subsequently more expensive to book. So if this mobile phone sponsored event is one of the last bastions of live entertainment that can afford to invite so many of them to play over one weekend, then that's just fine and dandy for the average indie, rock and pop kid.

Many exceptional performances by a heap of exceptional artists over the years mean that this event has become one of the UK's most famous festivals since first launching in 1996.

Okay, so V might not be the number one choice for a spiritually enhanced, bohemian hippy love-in. It's crowded, there's little space to spread out, the VIP bar fills with orange-faced celebrities and it's über corporate. On the other hand, if you're a huge fan of artists such as

Ian Brown, Radiohead, Pulp, Muse, Blur, Coldplay, Chemical Brothers or The Strokes then get thee to thy phone or computer and be quick to grab a ticket. Just remember that the bars are an awfully long way from the stages, so if you can't face trying to wind your way back through the masses to the front of the crowd you'll need to find a good spot at the back for easy beer runs.

The celeb-count is high at V (on the stages alone), anyone familiar with the pages of glossy mags can spend a good hour or two on the A-list lookout. Away from the main stages super-fun smaller tents with slippery wood-decking dancefloors are great for a boogie. Side-attractions such as giant-sized computer games, pampering Fashion Shows for the ladies, a Sessions Stage showcasing new acts and night time films (screened when the music finishes at 11pm) are golden extras.

WHEN Late August
GUIDE PRICE Approximately £145 for a weekend pass with camping, £125 for a weekend pass without camping and £70 day ticket.
CAPACITY 90,000 at V Chelmsford and 85,000 at V Staffordshire
CAMPING There's room for 53,000 campers at Chelmsford and 75,000 at

V Fesitval held over the same weekend at Weston Park. The latter lets campers in on the Thursday. Tangerine Fields offer luxury camping for the 5-star campers.
TOP TIP Tickets sell out super-fast, but if you do miss out at least you can catch the highlights on TV.

LIKE THAT, THEN YOU'LL LOVE
The FIB Heineken Benicàssim Festival (www.fiberfib.com) near Valencia in Spain promises sun, sea, big-name acts, late-night raves and camping.
LOCATION Hylands Park, Chelmsford and Weston Park, Weston-under-Lizard, Staffordshire

www.vfestival.com

The World Of Music, Arts and Dance was created by pop superstar Peter Gabriel in the early eighties. The first festival appeared at Somerset's Bath & West Showground near Shepton Mallet in 1982, and included such disparate acts as Echo & The Bunnymen and the Drummers of Burundi. Although anyone who was there still speaks of it in reverential tones, the inaugural WOMAD was badly attended and proved a financial flop. However, the seeds had been sewn for the UK's first and biggest world music festival, and it has successfully grown with each passing year.

In 2007 it relocated from its base at the Rivermead Centre in Reading and moved back to the countryside. Its current venue is Charlton Park, a private estate owned by the Earl of Suffolk and boasting 280 acres of parkland. Located just outside the historic Abbey town of Malmesbury in Wiltshire, it's twice the size of the previous site, so offers a much larger playing field for festival fun and frolics. This has been a relief for the many regular WOMADians who felt that the Reading site was becoming too cramped for them to properly let their hair down. And as long as the number of attendees doesn't escalate too much, there will be significantly more space and comfort for everyone (and little chance of sound bleed from the stages) to enjoy.

Following 2007's wet year, nicknamed WOMUD, the 2008 event was a great success. The sun shone and the new estate's potential was finally realised. Stalls and world food eateries are situated in and around the main area instead of in just one market place. Everything looks very colourful, with flags flying, people wearing silly hats and drums and interesting world sounds belting out around every corner.

There are four principal stages, three of which are situated in the main arena. The smaller BBC Radio 3 Stage isn't too far away, set in a little glade in the wooded Arboretum, not far from the enticingly named World Of Wellbeing quarter. A further stone's throw away is the multifaceted World Of Kids area, amusing the nippers while you're getting down to a spot of Nigerian Afro-beat. But if that doesn't do it for them the Steam Fair is sure to put big smiles on young faces.

Camping is also good, with decent-sized family areas and camper van spaces. Everything you would expect facility-wise is available. There are also large car parking areas, but you may have to trek quite a distance with your tent. Drumming in the campsite is the organisers' main bone of contention. It's not allowed after 8pm and if folks ignore this rule they'll be upsetting the licensing issues, so be warned.

WOMAD definitely feels a bit more on the posh side at its Wiltshire home, but then no one really misses the evenings at the Rivermead Centre when the club nights ended up feeling like a slightly sinister school disco, with a surreal mixture of hippies, crusties and locals eyeing each other nervously.

Now, anyone looking for DJ activity just has to seek out the humming San Frans Disco Bar. In 2008 WOMAD also hosted a drum 'n' bass event – Beat Bristol – in a 2,000-capacity marquee headlined by Roni Size. Balkan beat pioneers Shantel and the Bucovina Club Orkestar played on one of the main stages, as did On U Sound's Adrian Sherwood, so global dance music is also represented admirably.

An attitude devoid of any confrontation pervades the atmosphere here; the greatest draw of WOMAD really is its appeal to people of all ages and cultures. Long may this continue.

WHEN Late July
GUIDE PRICE Weekend tickets are £125 for adults; teenagers (14–17) pay £60; and 13s and under go free. Each adult can take two children free but it's £10 for each extra child thereafter.
CAPACITY 25,000
CAMPING A Park and Camp ticket (£50) allows you to park your car within 10 metres of your tent so long as each passenger holds a valid weekend ticket. It's a requirement of the licence that no drums are played between 8pm and 8am in the campsite.
TOP TIP You'll hear a lot of lyrics sung in foreign languages, so brush up on your linguistic skills before you go.
LIKE THAT, THEN YOU'LL LOVE The new 15,000-capacity 'international' music (as well as comedy and spoken word) festival called Heavenly Planet (www.heavenlyplanetfestival.co.uk), co-run by WOMAD's ex-artistic director Thomas Brooman, takes place back in the old Reading Rivermead site.
LOCATION Charlton Park, Malmesbury, Wiltshire SN16 9DG

www.womad.org

wychwood

Wychwood is a curious mix of contrasts. Those who go rave about its safe, family-friendly environment. Situated on a racecourse confined within the track itself, it's like being on a gigantic rec' but there's nowhere for the kids to run off to. Yet despite a prevailing conservative atmosphere, the line-up can be as varied and verging on the cutting-edge as the next festival.

Wychwood is a grown-up gathering of sensible, appreciative music fans who will watch a selection of folk, pop and rock and find something good to say about every act.

Expect to see a mix of suburban commuters, young couples and multi-generational families in the audience.

The Divine Comedy, Fun Lovin' Criminals, the Levellers, The Proclaimers, Rodrigo Y Gabriella, Badly Drawn Boy and Afro Celt Sound System have strummed away at Wychwood since the festival began. There's also world music from India, Cuba and Africa, and inspiring choices from the Brit indie scene billed alongside leading lights in comedy in the Big Top – which has featured the talents of Josie Lawrence and Stephen Frost.

Even the camping at Wychwood is structured — organised into pitches so that everyone has an equally sized spot, with enough space around their tents to spread out. Handily, you can even park close to camp, unload, put up the tent and then take your car off to the car park. Starting a festival weekend couldn't get much simpler. Although now's probably a good time to point out that Wychwood actively encourages people to use the more environmentally friendly travel option of cycling and provides bike racks onsite.

WHEN Late May

GUIDE PRICE £110 for an adult weekend ticket (but you can also get day tickets), £85 for 12–18-year-olds and other concessions; under-12s go free and there is a disabled 2-for-1 ticket offer (£110); £30 per camper van.

CAPACITY 10,000

CAMPING Divided into four separate areas: family, quiet, general and easy access for disabled. The campsite is equipped with showers, café, shop and benefits from 24-hour security.

TOP TIP Fill your purse, this is a festival with unusual food stalls selling ostrich burgers and kangaroo.

LIKE THAT, THEN YOU'LL LOVE THIS Equally, quaintly twee and conservative (by this we mean it's not too hedonistic, which is good for families) is early July's The Cornbury Music Festival (www. cornburyfestival.com) on the edge of the Wychwood Forest in Oxfordshire.

LOCATION Cheltenham Racecourse, Prestbury Park, Cheltenham, Gloucestershire GL50 4SH

www.wychwoodfestival.com

festivals for kids

No longer does the 'be seen and not heard' rule apply with children. Not at festivals, anyway. As if watching adults let their hair down wasn't an education in itself, organisers have now given kids their own arenas to be let loose in.

Wychwood   p116

There can't be a festival much safer than one that's held within the confines of a racecourse track. Wychwood Music Festival prides itself on its conservative, family-friendly atmosphere. Parents get to enjoy themselves without worrying that their kids might see anything untoward (as is possible at the more pleasure-seeking festivals). You can drive onto the campsite, unload your gear and drive back to the car park – a brilliant perk that is unique to Wychwood. There's a wealth of fun and activity: toddlers joining in an Early Ears music class, while more adventurous ones try Bhangra dancing; older siblings can indulge in a little yoga before settling down to a story with the fabulous Roald Dahl Museum storytellers. With over 100 workshops across the weekend, the only energy kids should have left come bedtime, is enough to zip themselves into their sleeping bags. And there's no need to bring books from home for bedtime stories – just borrow one overnight from The Little Library.

WOMAD   camp bestival

shambala   paléo

Camp Bestival p24

A family-friendly version of Bestival (p22) on Dorset's beautiful Jurassic Coast, Camp Bestival is ideal for anyone who finds trekking to the Isle of Wight too much with children and camping gear in tow. That's not to say that the entertainment is in any way Bestival-lite; there's heaps of adult fun to be had, too (and we ought to point out that there are kids' activities at Bestival, as well as the fantastic ferry ride en route). It's just that here kids are everywhere: in the campsites, in the queues for the loos, causing buggy jams or roaming around every which way, overjoyed at being let loose in the fancy castle grounds. Basically, expect kids in surround sound, and excitable ones at that. Camp Bestival's debut was a good effort for a start-up festival. Parking next to the campsites allows kids to quickly get stuck into activities: building giant cardboard castles; African drumming; or taking a ballet or tap class. The Kids' Garden had a Big Top, with a dressing-up tent, bouncy castle, a Breastival Mother and Baby temple, the Insect Village and Circus, and a Punch and Judy Stall. Add to those, physics for the boffs, a jousting show and donkey rides – and its kidtastic credentials are sky high.

Shambala p80

Shambala's hold of the family market is growing ever stronger. Proud to not be 'a deckchair event', all ages are encouraged to jump in and actively participate. But what will the kids choose first? There are sand pits, crazy golf, tree nets in the woods, BMX ramps, 'guerrilla gardening' workshops, a roller disco and giant trampolines. Animation workshops are screened on the main stage on the Sunday, after a sound system towed by a tricycle leads a stream of fairies, pirates and various characters with their handmade *papier mâché* animal creations around the site in a parade. Warm lakeside hot tubs are a winner for all ages, as is the lakeside volleyball 'beach'. Should it drizzle, head to one of the big art-making tents or the performance space that features acts for or by the kids. Recently the festival joined an exchange art programme raising money for two African charities; the Malawi Education Project and Banule School Project. Most activities are just a hop, skip or a jump away from both the camping area and the car park. And in the family campsite there's a tiny Mama's Tent yurt for baby massages and baths, so even the tiniest punters feel well looked after.

camp bestival

wychwood

Paléo Festival Nyon   p184

Every day, an average of 1,200 children visit Paléo Festival Nyon and they have as much of a good time as their parents. Any child aged up to eight years can be left for free at the onsite nursery Luciole, which is situated in the shade and away from the crowd (only if they are mud-free, though). The nursery is decked out with a different cartoon theme each year and provides expert care staff and even magicians. Its hours are definitely more European, staying open until 10 or 11pm. Elsewhere, teenagers manage a Mielimélo play area for children aged 6–12 years in La Ruche, which is a performing space for street theatre and circus arts divided up into seven 'alveoli' – areas where a multitude of artists 'perform, surprise, fascinate and charm' all ages with theatrical, artistic, musical and often downright bizarre productions. Also onsite are Les Fête des Jeux outsized games, cartoon workshops and sketching sessions. In 2008, kids could build scarecrows from recycled materials that were then exhibited in the village of Denens – the Swiss capital of scarecrows, no less. Teenagers hang out at La Plage, which has a sandpit, palm trees, games, a non-alcoholic bar and plenty of space.

WOMAD   p112

You'd be hard pushed to find a more relaxed festival that appeals to such a broad cross-section of creeds and ages in the entire United Kingdom than WOMAD. It's also one of the most technicoloured festivals: flags and colorific costumes abound. Parents can leave their children for free at any of the World of Kids workshops teaching a wide curriculum: from graffiti art and making wooden instruments to storytelling and learning to play the didgeridoo. For the last day's grand finale, a group of musicians lead a kids-only, all-singing, all-marching parade to the main stage. The parenting charity, NCT, runs a tent where young mums can breast-feed and parents can change nappies in relative peace, while older children get to enjoy games galore. Young and old alike will delight at the oldeworlde charm of the steam fair, with helter-skelter, dodgems, merry-go-rounds, chair-o-planes and more. Choose between the quieter family campsite and, for an extra £50, the 5-star glitz of the Park and Camp area if you like your car nearby. And if you lose track of your little ones, head for the Found Children area where professional carers work round the clock.

WOMAD

shambala

From the central Victorian Market Hall, where cartoon sculptures are suspended from the ceiling, more than 190 stalls spill out around the stunning castle grounds and along the cobbled side streets, demonstrating exactly why the *Observer Food Magazine* calls this 'the Glastonbury of food festivals'.

The tiny, picture postcard town of Abergavenny, on the south-eastern edge of the Brecon Beacons National Park, provides a spectacular backdrop that helps attract tourists to this autumn feast in their droves.

Today's celebrity TV chefs encourage us to be increasingly inventive with our cooking. Being the next Jamie, Nigella or Gordon has become an attractive career option for youngsters and a creative hobby for the rest of us. If the sight of a copy of *Delicious* or *Sainsbury's Magazine* leaves you wide-eyed with delight, then you'll feel like all your Christmases have come at once at Abergavenny's food grotto.

Just ignore those pretentious types looking to reap dinner party kudos by hanging around the superchef guests (Clarissa Dickson Wright, Anthony Bourdain and Hugh Fearnley-Whittingstall), and you'll find this to be a family-friendly day out that simply celebrates the tastier side of life.

The festival's foremost aim is to promote the consumption of fresh produce. You can taste and buy an assortment of goodies ranging from venison salami and sushi to goat's milk fudge and local Wild Fig ice cream. Welsh breweries jollify the atmosphere with a fine array of ales, wines and cider. And for the kids, helping out at the wood-fired oven pizza demonstrations or sausage-making master classes might just inspire a few beautiful careers.

WHEN Late September
GUIDE PRICE Adult £4.50/£9 (day/weekend) and under-15s £1.50–2.50; Sunday and weekend family tickets are also available.
CAPACITY 30,000
CAMPING As featured in the *Cool Camping: Wales* book, Llanthony Priory (www.llanthony.co.uk) is a lovely gem buried in the mountains, 11 miles from Abergavenny.
TOP TIP If you only go for one day, make it the Saturday, because Saturday night is party night with live music and DJs at the castle.

LIKE THAT, THEN YOU'LL LOVE
Throw back some oysters at July's Whitstable Oyster Festival (www.whitstableoysterfestival.co.uk) on the 'pearl' of the Kent coast.
LOCATION Abergavenny, Monmouthshire, Wales

www.abergavennyfoodfestival.com

AMERICANA

Befittingly, considering the country's own bold mantras, Americana International is Europe's very own 'biggest and best American lifestyle event'. It's a sentiment shared by the thousands of committed fans who relive 80 years of US history over the course of one solitary weekend.

Americana International is, essentially, a car rally with bells on. In Nottinghamshire's County Showground, rows of classic cars, trucks and bikes dating from 1900 glow in all their original or customised glory. Inside the pavilions eight decades of US music ring out to the tune of spur-stinging country, quifftastic rockabilly, screaming hillbilly and jiving rock 'n' roll.

Over the best part of three decades, the event's popularity has exploded. Even the US Ambassador in London is a keen visitor. Conceived in a pub car park with just two bands and 80 cars as entertainment, it now ushers in 7,000 vehicles from all over the world, including Harley-Davidson and Indian motorcycles to '55 Chevys and 1970 Pontiac Firebirds. (*American Beauty*'s Lester Burnham would never have had a mid-life crisis if he'd had all this excitement happening on his doorstep!)

Dressing up and getting into character is par for the course. Native American Indians, cowboys and cheerleaders are the most popular fancy dress outfits; and the site is strewn with more stars and stripes than you can shake a Stetson at. Some women adopt 1950s housewife personas, while their hubbies patrol as uniformed police officers. A handful of couples go so far as to construct their own wooden shacks to sleep in, living out their *Little House on the Prairie* fantasies – bonnets, porches, rocking chairs and all.

WHEN Early/mid July
GUIDE PRICE Adult £80 plus £25 per camping unit. Under-15s accompanied by an adult are free.
CAPACITY 30,000
CAMPING There are two areas but you need to pre-book because they fill up quickly. Wigwam tents are popular, and there is space for 14,000 – sometimes quite huge – American motor homes.
TOP TIP Live the American Dream without having to fly over the Atlantic. In the US, nobody bats an eyelid if you want to dress as a cowboy, and nor will they here, so feel free to fully immerse yourself into character.
LIKE THAT, THEN YOU'LL LOVE Britain's fascination with VW camper vans can be indulged to the full at Run To The Sun (www.runtothesun.co.uk), a dance, music and comedy, family camping event held near Newquay, Cornwall, in May.
LOCATION The County Showground, Winthorpe, Newark, Nottinghamshire NG24 2NY

www.americana-international.co.uk

Buddhism originated as a nomadic religion, early practitioners seeking enlightenment would meet at natural, coppiced locations considering them to be ideal for harmonious meditation. Buddhafield Festival continues this tradition and moves from one arboured site to another every year. Meditation, reflection, and communication: the festival embraces all of these, with heaps of music and dancing on top.

The UK is home to over 150,000 practising Buddhists, a figure that is increasing with new styles emerging all the time. Buddhafield Festival is a branch of the Friends of the Western Buddhist Order, a school that practises the religion in a Western-friendly context – 'rules' are relaxed to adapt to our modern day-to-day lifestyles.

The festival is an alcohol-and-drug-free zone, with Chai tea the strongest brew on offer, but then that seems to be all the incentive most people need to rise at day break. Experienced Buddhists converge to meditate in one tent and the beginners and intermediates group together next door. Alternatively, you can always start the day with a capoeira class – a captivating Brazilian hybrid of martial arts and dance.

Morning activities are endless: join a lesson in yoga, salsa or Shamanic dancing; make jewellery; or sign up for a Thai massage workshop (alternatively, you can pay for a professional massage in the Healing Area). Afternoon activities feature debates on anything from social change to Tibetan singing classes. Dance DJs spin a mixture of trance-world, reggae and Bollywood records and two solar-powered music stages provide amplified music until 11pm, when acoustic bands take over, entertaining the blissed out Buddhists till early next morning.

WHEN Mid July
GUIDE PRICE £85 for adults, 11s and over are £30 and kids (2–10) cost £15. It's £75 for concessions. Car parking passes are a whopping £18.
CAPACITY 2,500
CAMPING All camping is situated near to cafés, and the fields are surrounded by woodland. There are donation wood-fired showers and compost loos.
TOP TIP Buddhafield also runs several Devon camping retreats throughout the year. Up to four-dozen guests of all ages and levels of experience meditate, walk, cook and eat (vegetarian food) together.

LIKE THAT, THEN YOU'LL LOVE From one religion to another, One Love Music Festival (www.onelovefestival. co.uk) worships at the altar of Bob Marley every August. Dub and reggae are the mainstays of this East Sussex event.
LOCATION Somewhere near Taunton, Somerset

www.buddhafield.com

fringe

Every August, Edinburgh's population doubles in size as one million people squeeze in for the world's largest arts festival, the International Edinburgh Festival. Since launching in 1947 it has increased in popularity with every passing year. While sunshine in Scotland may be a rare occurrence, even at the height of summer, the festival does a fine job of warming up the capital city for three long, happy weeks.

'Edinburgh Festivals' is a mesmerising celebration of the arts that includes opera, theatre and dance, jamborees for books, a little jazz and, until recently, film screenings. The best-known single element, though, is the Edinburgh Fringe Festival. It offers a mix of modern and experimental theatre and comedy, the latter of which only recently became the festival's main focus and is now a teeming hotbed of comedy talent. The if.comedy award-nominated comedian Andrew Maxwell best described the Fringe as 'exams for clowns' and according to Jimmy Carr, the process is like doing 'a PhD in comedy'.

Among the many venues now tickling our funny bones is a grouping known as 'The Big 4': The Pleasance, The Underbelly, The Assembly Rooms and The Gilded Balloon. In 2008, this gaggle of venues launched The Edinburgh Comedy Festival, a controversial fringe festival within the Fringe. Don't feel too confused, because the only real difference of the new spin-off so far has been the appearance of yet another brochure to add to the collection in your bag.

A smaller venue definitely worth discovering is The Stand – a year-round club on York Place favoured by cult acts like Stewart 'Jerry Springer the Opera' Lee, Andy Zaltzman and Daniel Kitson, who has performed stand up there exclusively since 2004. There's also The Free Fringe that does what it says on the (collection) tin and is a great option if you are aiming to see a lot of shows.

Booking is advisable so become acquainted with the official website for details and gen up on profiles before you go. Often the most popular acts will put on an extra show, but if you can't get tickets for those, watch out for the multi-bill cabaret nights that take place around midnight at most of the venues. Also well worth attending are the if.comedy award shows on the final weekend – they're the equivalent to the Oscars for comedians, but without the Hollywood pomp, ceremony and botox.

With drink prices that give London a run for its money, the cost of revelry can be high in Edinburgh. Though you are unlikely to find fancy whiskies at Fringe bars, the later you are out, the more you'll probably drink and eat. But don't worry about gaining a few extra pounds (on top of the many you spend), as you'll soon walk them all off. The attractions tend to be evenly split between both sides of town so there's a fair bit of criss-crossing to do. And if you don't walk them off, you'll sweat them off in the various venues that are often small, hot, but wonderfully atmospheric; the intimacy is part of what makes the spirit of the Fringe, so don't forget to pack your deodorant.

If you're there for the entire festival and don't want to get too fringed out, give yourself a breather by walking up to Arthur's Seat, the large hill to the east of the city. Otherwise, enjoy some fresh air at The Firth of Forth estuary to the north. Sit down with a sandwich in the garden area by The Spiegeltent where burlesque-style cabaret takes place throughout the day. Just a short walk from there lies The Meadows, also offering much needed respite from the busy city streets.

Now, breathe in deeply, and off you go again... Jump straight back into the fray to start studying hard for that PhD. When you return home, your repetition of tall tales and legendary laughs may well encourage a few friends to come along for the ride next year.

WHEN Three weeks in August, ending on the bank holiday weekend.
GUIDE PRICE Various venues spread throughout Edinburgh's fair city. Prices vary from £5 to £15 per show; The Free Fringe shows are, you guessed it, free. The Fringe Office is a one-stop-shop for information on tickets, venues and performers.
CAPACITY Around 500,000 visitors turn up for the Edinburgh Festivals each year.
TOP TIP Grab a meal at the unofficial 'food garden', next door to The Gilded Balloon and then indulge in some celeb spotting at the Library Bar.

LIKE THAT, THEN YOU'LL LOVE
A fifth of the size, Festival d'Avignon (www.festival-avignon.com) is a three-week-long French arts affair with a less hedonistic bent, in July in the south of France.
LOCATION Edinburgh, Midlothian, Scotland

www.edfringe.com

HAY FESTIVAL

Described by Bill Clinton as 'the Woodstock of the mind', this most cultured of festivals sees a massive array of talent pour itself into the picturesque town of Hay-on-Wye, snuggled at the bottom of the Black Mountains, in the Brecon Beacons National Park. For 10 days in late spring/early summer, this town plays host to the annual *Guardian* Hay Festival – a right old literary knees-up.

Hay, also (unofficially) known as 'book town', boasts more bookshops than residents. Okay, that's not strictly true; it had around 40 bookshops at last count and 2,500 residents, but that does make it the town with the biggest concentration of literature in the UK and the perfect destination for budding bibliophiles. This king of all literary festivals has spawned dozens of boutique imitators since launching in 1987, including the Hay's own forays abroad, in Spain and Columbia (the newest, Mapfre Hay Festival Alhambra, opened in Granada in 2008 showcasing Tunisian music, Spanish gastronomy, Arabic literature and chess championships).

Despite its modest size and relatively rural location, the Hay Festival succeeds in attracting literary big-hitters; controversial author Salman Rushdie, left-wing intellectual Naomi Klein or contemporary novelists such as Marian Keyes and Will Self, for instance, have all been visitors in recent years. It's an opportunity for readers and fans to get up close to their favourite writers and grill them on plots, characters and opinions. While the event is primarily a gathering of writers, comedians and literati creative types, in recent years it has emerged as a hotbed of musical talent too. Half a dozen live acts perform, with the likes of Macy Gray, Debbie Harry and Hot Chip pulling in a younger crowd.

The festival site itself sits in peaceful pastures on the outskirts of Hay, a pretty market town graced with Norman ruins. A compact village of tented stages are linked by AstroTurf walkways, broken up with numerous posh nosh stalls and covered bars – although most people tend to drink in the cheaper local pubs in the town centre. An Edinburgh-style fringe festival runs alongside the main event, showcasing an array of engaging musical talent all over the town. These low-key gigs take place in bookshop basements, social clubs and, well, any tiny cubby hole you can squeeze an acoustic guitar-toting folkie into.

After a hard day of mingling with the intelligentsia, stumbling across impromptu gigs and poetry recitals, and whiling away the hours with the day's newspapers and a luxury locally made ice cream, you will want somewhere peaceful to lay your head. The official campsite, Tangerine Fields, is situated a mile or so from the festival and is a perfect place to relax. You can bring your own tent or book one of the pre-erected dome constructions, which come kitted out with blown-up airbeds, plump pillows and sleeping bags (these are donated to Oxfam and Crisis after the event).

For those seeking a more adventurous sleeping spot there are a number of other campsites within easy strolling distance of the site, including the Hollybush Inn and Campsite. Here, perched over the River Wye, you can spread out in the shady woodland or in the rugged fields where regal peacocks roam free.

An inn at the top of the campsite serves up fresh, home-cooked food, local real ales and ciders as well as a weird and wonderful range of rural wines.

Festival debauchery this is not; you are more likely to be kept up all night by a heated game of Scrabble in the tent next door than the banging beats of a sound system. But come summer's end when you're reliving favourite festival memories – the time you caught the latest in underground anti-folk in a tatty bookstore before hearing an eminent literary heavyweight make insightful observations about the poetic resonance of the former Eastern Block might well top your list.

WHEN Late May
GUIDE PRICE Most events are £5–19 and are free for students.
CAPACITY Around 95,000 visitors over 10 days.
CAMPING Onsite, there's boutique camping with dome tents for hire, courtesy of Tangerine Fields (www.tangerinefields.co.uk). Otherwise, Hollybush Inn and Campsite (www.hollybushcamping.co.uk) accommodates around 2,500 guests over the weekend (£6 per person per night) and they rent five tipis and two yurts (£12.50 per person per night) on their 22 acres. They provide and sell meals here and you can either walk into Hay or hire canoes to paddle the one-hour journey along the river (the campsite bosses will then come and collect the canoe).
TOP TIP Breathe in fantastic panoramas by climbing up to the top of Hay Bluff (over 600 metres high), which looks north over towards Hay with the Radnorshire Hills beyond. Walkers can divert back on to the Offa's Dyke trail from here.
LIKE THAT, THEN YOU'LL LOVE As literary camping festivals go, you'll be hard pushed to beat the Port Eliot Festival (www.porteliotfestival.com) held in Cornwall in late July.
LOCATION The Drill Hall, 25 Lion Street, Hay-on-Wye, Herefordshire HR3 5AD

www.hayfestival.com

eco

friendly festivals

Not that long ago, calls to cleanse the world ethically and environmentally were ignored by all but the new-age hippies. Not so any more. Global warming has become the *sujet du jour* and some festivals are keener than most to roll up their sleeves and help save the planet.

Sunrise Celebration   p84

When it began in 2006, it was the first UK festival to use eco loos. They ran a competition to find a new design and their new self-built 'deluxe' models now have doors and willow trees grow out of the compost. All the festival's stages are powered by 100 per cent renewable energy (solar, cycle and wind power), except for the main stage, which is too big and so is run off a biodiesel generator. Sunrise works with SolarAid, a charity committed to combating poverty and climate change through the use of solar power, and Blooming Futures, a leading environmental group that promotes sustainable biofuels and presses vegetable oil onsite to power an entire arena. Borrowing the ethos of Totnes Town Transition Network, Sunrise promotes the use of local resources within communities. So regional, organic food is served on compostable plates and all working areas are cleaned with eco products. Even the graffiti artists work with special paints and use compressors instead of aerosols.

sunrise celebration

2000 trees

beachdown

isle of wight

Give Bees a chance
Give us your Money

All money from the Bee Bin goes
towards Island Bee conservation

MONEY
ONLY
PLEASE!

Give Bees a chance
Give us your Money

All money from the Bee Bin goes
towards Island Bee conservation

The 2000 Trees Festival p104

Originally, organisers intended to plant a tree for each one of the 2,000 guests who attended their first festival. When that became financially unviable, they decided to stick with the title anyway. Sweeping, leafy vistas of Gloucestershire and a nature trail from the campsite to Upcote Plantation presents a scene no one could possibly wish to spoil. To combat any rogue littering, the Maker Green tidy-up Team keeps the site spotless, recycling and composting whatever they can. According to Network Recycling, the average UK recycling rate at festivals is only 30 per cent, and the Maker Green Team achieved 75 per cent in 2008. Stages and lights are run on locally sourced biodiesel oil, and the Greenhouse DJ shed is painted green in support of their overall environmental policy. Students and lecturers from the University of Aston give renewable energy demonstrations (one such topic covered the use of pedal-powered mobile phone chargers). Food is locally produced and served in biodegradable containers, and in 2010 organisers intend to trial a solar-powered stage. The festival's strict UK-only booking policy means no carbon emissions are racked up flying talent in from overseas, scoring masses of green stars.

Beachdown p14

This event gets a head start due to its location alone. With so many Sussex-based seasoned festival veterans snapping up most of the tickets, there are less to sell to carbon-emitting long-distance travellers. Beachdown transport is green and easy. Shuttle buses run from the seafront and railway station (so festival goers need not bring their cars) to the festival site 20 minutes away on the South Downs. The fleet is powered by used cooking oil, and hired from The Big Lemon bus company (Brighton's own eco-transport system, which prospers from having a local biodiesel filling station in the city). At the festival, every drop of biodiesel, water, cocktail and beer is measured and project managed by the independent charity drop4drop, with the assistance of a locally based bottled water company, Life Pure Water, so that the equivalent amount of water (100,000 litres in 2008) is donated to sustainable water projects in Uganda and Malawi. All the food at Beachdown is organic and supplied by local caterers and traders. The festival also encourages a strict Leave No Trace tidy-up strategy that's proved hugely successful at The Big Chill (p90) and America's famous Burning Man event where the ethos originated.

beachdown

sunrise celebration

Isle of Wight

When Lily Allen had to cancel her performance in 2008, rather than line an alternative artist's pocket with the savings, festival boss John Giddens invested the cash in an Eco-Action Team that could audit the festival's carbon footprint. Two research funds were set up, one to repopulate the island's indigenous black poplar trees and another, the 'Give Bees a Chance' campaign (nothing to do with the Isle of Wight's most famous band The Bees, incidentally!) to save the island's waning bee population, which has been hit by depleting hedgerows and a disease linked to pesticides. The local council's Environmental Health division is working alongside partners to turn the Isle of Wight into a fully sustainable 'Eco Island' by 2020. Home installation systems are to be tackled first, with an £8 million gasification plant that will generate enough power to heat 2,000 homes. In line with this progressive philosophy, the festival has embarked upon a five-year strategy that began with charging for car parking and offering bikes for hire at the ferry ports. Used cooking oil will be collected by the new Defra-funded waste-to-energy plant on the island and aluminium cans will be used to boost certain schools' funding.

Boom

Boom takes place every two years during the August full moon in a tribute to historic ceremonies that celebrated cycles of the earth, moon and sun. Constantly striving towards sustainability, this festival's philosophy is that people 'share with each other and care for the Earth'. A Greener Festival presented Boom with an international award and 'outstanding' status for its ecological work (festivals are judged on categories from event and waste management, travel and transport, greenhouse gas emissions and fair-trade). Recycled ashtrays are dished out and dry compost toilets – their black chambers enable the sun to turn compost into manure – are generously provided. The used water from all the festival's restaurants, bars and showers is recycled onsite using a biological treatment self-cleaning system, and guests are urged to limit their water use. They're also encouraged to bring any used vegetable oil to help power the generators. Festival waste matter is deposited into a conversion facility that compacts it into organic fertiliser. Such is Boom's eco conviction that anyone caught littering the UNESCO Geopark Naturtejo site will probably be put on one of the lift-sharing Boom Buses and sent home.

unrise celebration

boom

The historic image of stocky, hirsute Vikings charging through battalions like tidal battering rams isn't a trait that has entirely diminished among their Icelandic descendants.

To be clearer, if you're used to attending large-scale music gigs, you'll be accustomed to snaking your way through dense crowds. At Iceland Airwaves, sometimes you've just got to hold on tightly to your drink, because when these young natives decide they want a better view of the stage – WHALLOP! – walking directly ahead through a standing crowd, they'll send you (and your drink) flying.

But it's nothing personal. Turning around and flashing a wide smile, these proud Viking descendants are forgiven, even for spilling our credit-crunch-defying vodka. Add to their friendly, pixie-faced welcome the country's fresh, unpolluted air; fjords and waterfalls, Bond-style snowmobile excursions across glacial landscapes; whales and dolphins on their Arctic adventures; and spiralling Northern Lights, then throw in five days and nights of cutting-edge bands and you'd be mad not to book your ticket this very instant.

Dress for the icy winds and head for the Skífan record store to pick up a *Reykjavík Grapevine* paper and festival programme. Reykjavík is not large for a capital city so you're unlikely to get lost, just head downtown to get stuck into the Airwaves action. The Reykjavík Art Museum (Iceland's own Tate Modern), the massive NASA nightclub and the artier Barinn are where the bigger acts play. Most of the artists on the bill are Icelandic or Scandinavian. For every Sigur Rós, GusGus and Emiliana Torrini there's a lesser-known but popular home-grown name such as Retro Stefson, Dr. Spock or Sudden Weather Change playing in any one of the 22 official and unofficial venues.

Hot dogs sell like, well, hot dogs, in the city centre. Everyone's eating them. That's probably because most cafés sell them, and this is where festival-goers spend daylight hours watching acoustic sets, in between visits to the museum to hear various industry talks.

For a refreshing change of scenery head to Iceland's iconic hotspot, the Blue Lagoon. The festival organises an expedition on the Saturday, when you can hear DJs play lounge music from the comfort of the sulphuric steam springs. It isn't included in the ticket price, so you could go under your own steam, as it's a great place to chill, even without the Airwaves crew.

In the evenings, the streets may look lifeless but that's just because it's so cold outside. Turn a corner and suddenly you'll see several thousand people clamouring outside the museum for a piece of the headline band. If you can't face the queues, then the mini '70s-retro Organ bar, or Iðnó (an old theatre that's been transformed into a hip venue) by the Tjörnina lake are good bets for discovering vibey bands.

When the programmed music stops, the party doesn't end there. This geographic wonder of a country only became independent in 1944, and as a small population (just over 300,000), Icelanders enjoy socialising as much as their international guests do, so they'll think nothing of inviting tourists to tag along with them to random house parties.

In 2008 the 10th Iceland Airwaves took place just days after the country declared itself bankrupt. In their pre-printed programmes, the festival's director, Thorsteinn Stephensen, expressed disappointment in the government's concentrated investments in theatre and film, while their domestic pool of musical talent remained under-nurtured. Perhaps this will change. What can't be disputed is that this superb event has done as much as their greatest star, Björk, to promote Iceland to the world in its own unique, and rather boisterous, voice.

WHEN Late October
GUIDE PRICE 8,900 krónur for a five-day pass to various venues across Reykjavík works out approximately at a bargain £50. You can also purchase day tickets or buy your pass as part of a package deal with Icelandair when you purchase your flights.
CAPACITY 8,000 daily.
CAMPING Unfortunately, all the campsites close in September, but there are plenty of cheap, warm B&Bs to choose from.

TOP TIP Dig into traditional cuisine such as reindeer steak, smoked lamb or puffin breast. Also, horse-riding is a must. The Icelandic horse breed dates back to the Viking invasion, and boasts a unique smooth-flowing tölt (running walk). Enjoy the sensation of flying through the air in your saddle, while admiring Iceland's stunning scenery. Regular trips are organised by the tourist office (Adalstraeti 2, 101 Reykjavík; 00 354 590 1550; www.visitreykjavik.is).

LIKE THAT, THEN YOU'LL LOVE
Equally bracing is Øya Festival (www.oyafestivalen.com), a three-stage, four-day music festival on the outskirts of Oslo, set around a small lake with views of the city's skyline. Norwegian acts haven't yet matched Röyksopp, their best music export to date, but you'll discover the odd band among a host of international talent to get excited about.
LOCATION Downtown Reykjavík (for info: Airwaves Information Centre, Skífan, Laugavegur 26, 101 Reykjavík)

www.icelandairwaves.com

LOVEBOX

When is a festival not a festival? When it's in a city park; when you can't camp out under the stars; when the sound volumes are controlled by local residents...So then, technically speaking, Lovebox isn't a festival. But since when were festivals about conforming to definitions of 'the norm'? Lovebox's head honchos, including dance music stars Groove Armada and live music giants, the London-based MAMA Group, confidently pull off a blinder of an event — in one of the world's greatest capitals — that ticks a good many of our festival boxes.

Hop off the tube at one of three stations (or off any one of several buses passing this way) and follow the crowds heading towards Victoria Park in Hackney. Approaching the entrance, you'll witness a palpable excitement building at the gates. All these early arrivals want is to get inside and get going. They know that after warming up with a little live main stage music, then sipping their way around the cocktail bars and shaking their rumps at various creative dance spaces, it'll already be late-afternoon and there's still half a festival to explore.

Sonically, Lovebox keeps in step with London's fast-paced music trends, and all tastes are catered for. Plenty of big name bands have celebrated a retro flavour; artists like Blondie,

Sly & the Family Stone and The Human League have all graced the main stage in recent years, fuelling public singalongs on a massive scale. At the other end of the music spectrum, among the smaller sound systems that are tucked away in tents or hidden behind trees, both The Great Escape and *Clash* magazine stages present the finest up-and-coming bands. In the fenced circle that is The Copse rave den and at the New York-style enclave on the edge of the park, underground stalwarts secretsundaze and the Downlow DJ hosts respectively bash out beats and disco exhibitionism to make the capital's hedonists steam up behind their sunglasses.

There's no let up in quality music, even if the volume is never whacked up to full blast (because of those nearby residents). And for many people who go, Lovebox is also about eating their way through the range of delicious food stalls fresh from Borough Market. From hog roasts to coconuts, oysters to quality burgers — you can easily lose a few hours here. Add to the food: fairground rides, graffiti walls, make-up trucks, bars, swooshing flags, balloons (Lovebox has always been big on balloons) — and undisputedly a magical 'festival' atmosphere does exist. Maybe you would struggle to find a hippy here, but there are enough clubbers, families, world music fans and OK yes, policemen too, to create one hugely diverse crowd.

With 35,000 people to water, feed and avail themselves of the portaloos you should expect to queue for pretty much everything. Although, despite these numbers, getting close to the main stage isn't impossible, which is handy because nabbing yourself a spot close to the front speakers is a good idea if you're here for the music.

At 10pm everything stops. This being London, it's not hard to carry on partying. Everyone streams out of the park to overflow every bus, minicab and tube train within a two-mile radius. On the Saturday night, hundreds will head to official 'after parties', many go to private house parties and only a very few will go home to sleep. Whatever they choose to do, the savvy ones will be back when the gates open on Sunday for another – albeit more chilled – day of Lovebox entertainment.

WHEN Mid July
GUIDE PRICE From £59
CAPACITY 35,000 daily
TOP TIP Plan both your exit and your after-party itinerary to beat the crowds, 35,000 people pouring out of the park at once requires some patience if you're grabbing a bus or a place on the tube. Also, there's nowhere to park a car at or near Victoria Park, so don't drive. People are searched as they enter the site, so smuggling in drinks is a no-no.
LIKE THAT, THEN YOU'LL LOVE Another London biggie is dance weekender SouthWestFour (www. southwestfour.com) with international trance DJ-gods and breaks lynchpins Fingerlickin'. It's held over the Saturday and Sunday of August's bank holiday weekend (so you'll have Monday off to recover).
LOCATION Victoria Park, Hackney, London E9

sónar

The Sónar stable caters for all sorts – those who prefer partying under the sun and those who only emerge after dusk. Whatever the time of day there's always music pouring out of Barcelona's various venues. Six operate through the day (SónarVillage, SónarHall, SónarDôme...) and four at night (also pre-fixed with Sónar, so you know where you're at) providing visitors with entertainment around the clock.

For fans of new, electronic music the programming is second to none (see Festivals for New Music, p160). Ultra-hip up-and-coming producers and bands (2008 highlights included Hercules And Love Affair, Flying Lotus, Little Dragon and Diplo) rub shoulders with electro superstars (Richie Hawtin, Miss Kittin and Ed Banger Records are regulars) at label showcases, arena shows and other in-the-know intimate spots in the city.

Beyond the official events there is plenty of fringe action to be hunted down. Venues all over the city play host to special club nights; so on top of the already extensive festival programme, there are pre-parties, after-parties and alternative parties to choose between, including La Terrazza's Sunday afternoon gathering featuring London's secretsundaze DJs.

A late night on the Catalan tiles is followed by a late rise, then a ramble around the cobbled city streets to choose the ideal spot for a late lunch of calamari and cold beer (do watch

out for pickpockets though). Music kicks off at midday, but the best way to spend afternoons is sprawled out on the lawns of the Sónar Village, digesting your tapas while watching the new – and sometimes quite bizarre – musical goings-on.

A more perfect setting for a city festival such as this is tough to find; with a happening nightlife worth exploring all year round, Barcelona has bars, restaurants and culture at every turn. Sónar has made this already vibrant European city even more so.

WHEN Mid June
GUIDE PRICE €140 for a weekend ticket; €30 for a day; €40 for the opening night; and €48 for all other nights.
CAPACITY 12,000 by day and 25,000 by night
CAMPING People hire apartments or stay in hotels, as the nearest campsites are some distance away.

With everything that's going on and the chance that friendly faces will insist on taking you from one party to the next, you're probably better off staying as near as you can within the city.
TOP TIP Don't expect to get much rest – you'll be too busy zigzagging your way from venue to venue sampling sangria and tapas along the way. Also, don't be surprised to join the end of big

queues if you turn up too late for the popular acts.
LIKE THAT, THEN YOU'LL LOVE Monegros (www.monegrosfestival.com) is a desert festival situated halfway between Madrid and Barcelona. The Spanish come here to party in mid July.
LOCATION Various venues across Barcelona, Spain

www.sonar.es

T IN THE PARK

We first played T in 2003 when we were very much a new band. We drove up from Glasgow, crammed into the back of a transit van. We were stopped by security on the way in and had to argue with them for hours to persuade them that, honest, we were supposed to be playing... The following year, T In the Park was our first live gig back in Scotland since playing in Glasgow just after the first album came out five months before. We'd been all round the planet playing, and we were wondering, are folk back home gonna be into it? And it was one of the best gigs of my life. Looking out over the brow of the hill, all I could see were people jumping up and down, going absolutely crazy, undulating like an ocean in a storm. It was the most spine-tingling moment. I've got more memories of T from being in other bands as well. In 1989 I opened up the festival with The Amphetameanies. We were just a wee band and there we were on the main stage, with Joe Strummer saying hello. T in the Park is great that way: it's a big international festival now but there is still a strong support for the Scottish music scene. And you have those completely uninhibited crowds – unselfconscious and not embarrassed about going wild and having the greatest time of their lives. It's seen as a real special event, a getaway, a party for the whole country. People go with the best possible attitude, and you can really feel that when you're standing on stage.

ALEX KAPRANOS
SINGER, FRANZ FERDINAND

For three days in July the bars, courtyards and warehouses of Birmingham's famous Custard Factory host the independent, multi-tendrilled musical beast that is Supersonic, discharging sounds quite unlike any you'll hear elsewhere.

Supersonic has a distinctive roar that can be heard all over the West Midlands and beyond. Recalling the city's musical history, Birmingham's heavy metal, grindcore, twisted techno and dirty drum 'n' bass are prime components of this experimental music convention.

Friday night is a raucous party night, with a host of international live acts and DJs playing hip-hop to electronica via punk rock. On Saturday, the Custard Factory's outdoor yard becomes home to a few live music stages where acts from all corners of the earth perform anything from grime to beautiful, eerie folk music.

An indoor theatre space schedules various lectures, films, intimate performances and debates that celebrate and dissect alternative culture. Brightening up the urban courtyard are onstage projections and art installations. Graffiti spills over from canvases in the indoor gallery's exhibition and all over the site itself. At night, the 2,000-capacity Medicine Bar is where the party goers really let their hair down.

Supersonic champions marginal and extreme music. Its innovative programming has earned the festival the utmost respect worldwide during its seven-year reign. Organisers, Capsule, select bands and DJs that are generally ahead of the curve – for instance, New York four-piece Battles played here before the 'math rock' sound had really surfaced. And a future guest wish-list includes biggies like American sludge metal band the Melvins and Birmingham's most famous heavy metal band, Black Sabbath.

WHEN Mid July
GUIDE PRICE Approx £65 for the weekend; Friday ticket £15, Saturday £35 and Sunday £30.
CAPACITY 2,500
TOP TIP Read up on Plan B or The Wire magazines so you don't feel like a stranger to Supersonic's more experimental sounds. Onsite, show your support for independent record labels by buying their wares – a dozen of them (Southern Records, Static Caravan, Rough Trade and more) have their own merchandise stalls, situated in the festival's Market Place.
LIKE THAT, THEN YOU'LL LOVE All Tomorrow's Parties (www.atpfestival.com) host weekend events for dedicated musos at various holiday centres. Equally specialist, their avant-garde line-ups are curated by respected musicians (such as the Melvins). Tickets are like gold dust.
LOCATION The Custard Factory, Gibb Square, Digbeth, Birmingham B9 4AA

www.capsule.org.uk/supersonic

synch

Since winning the bid in 1997 to host the 2004 Olympic Games, Athens hasn't looked back. It was the homecoming event of the millennium, a celebration of the inaugural Games in 1896 and a beacon of a brighter, prosperous future. The construction of new transport infrastructures to cope with the international visitors was the lifeline Athens needed to reinvent itself as a modern city.

Although many of the sporting arenas have since become derelict, everywhere else in the city feels spruced up. You could say that aspiring Athenians grabbed the Olympic baton and sprinted into a brand new world. Now that the city is finding its place in Europe, it is no longer just a stopgap for holidaymakers on their way to the Greek islands. During the hot summer months, the capital buzzes with good-looking guys and girls socialising outside bars and cafés. People are stylishly dressed, and everyone at the festival seems so friendly; it's enough to make you want to move here.

Born on the island of Ikaria (named after Icarus, the mythological character who flew so close to the sun that his wings melted) project manager Giorgos Karnavas and music director Dimitri Papaioannou later met in Athens, and together dreamed up a festival that would showcase a diverse global programme of music, arts and new technology. Labelled a mini-version of Sónar (p148), the weekend features daytime debates, talks, short films, workshops and audio-visual installations at the high-tech Benaki Museum; then as night takes over, live music spreads across various stages at an old gasworks factory, the Technopolis industrial museum.

Home-grown artists and mixologists kick off proceedings in the museum's courtyard. A watching public more used to hiding indoors or under beach umbrellas seemed to wilt like un-watered houseplants in the sweltering afternoon sun in 2008 (fortunately organisers will be hooking up sheltered canopies at future daytime events). Still, the arena spurted with life the next day when the intriguing chamber music of Your Hand in Mine, and the Greek singer-songwriter Monika enticed the crowds out of the shade.

Bands come from all over Europe and America and so far have included The Liars, Holy Fuck and Fischerspooner, alongside the more electronica workings of The Field, DJ Pierre and Andrew Weatherall. Outdoor stages are rigged with top-notch sound systems (Giorgos' day job is production manager). Digital movies and short films showcase modern cinematography alongside highbrow audio-visual and art installations. There is indoor space to accommodate sweaty basement raves and a café, as well as the odd random spectacle, which recently included members of Masters of the Universe playing their instruments on top of five-metre-high wooden towers.

Beer queues can be long, made longer if you don't get the requisite tokens from the cabin across the site, but two extra bars are being installed – Greek summer partying is thirsty work. Huge, welcoming smiles fill the night, with sweaty indoor clubbing proving that you don't need to be a Greek myth to melt away.

Pace yourself, because when Technopolis finishes at 5am, the party is still going down the road. Head out of the main exit and along the tree-lit avenue, passing posh Mediterranean-style dining tables to Gazi, the bar and club area purpose-built in 2006. Inside the Yoga Bala, Motel, Bios and K44 clubs are a host of Synch DJs playing everything from techno to house, disco and electro until long after the sun has risen over the Acropolis, heralding a new day.

WHEN Mid June

GUIDE PRICE From €45 for a day pass to €80 for a three-day pass.

CAPACITY 7,000 daily

CAMPING See *Cool Camping: Europe* for the low down on Greek campsites, including Nicolas Camping (www. nicolasgikas.gr). Better to visit for a few days either side of the festival as it's two hours away from Athens, but it's an enchanting site where pitches are shaded by mulberry and orange trees,

so well worth a stay. During the festival take advantage of the many hostels and hotels the city has to offer.

TOP TIP Stay out late, sleep in, have a late lunch at the pedestrianised 'neighbourhood of the Gods' Plaka area, then do a little record shopping at 360 (Elasidon 29, Keramikos), an independent record store close to Synch before rejoining the festival.

LIKE THAT, THEN YOU'LL LOVE Italia Wave (www.italiawave.com) is a four-

day, clubbier dance music festival in July with literature, sport and various workshops on top, in the city of Livorno on Italy's Tuscan coast. There are campsites nearby and entry is free but access to the main football stadium arena and the Old Fortress in the evenings will set you back between €10 and €25.

LOCATION Benaki Museum, 138 Pireos Street and Technopolis, 100 Pireos Street, 11854 Athens, Greece

www.synch.gr

festivals for

new n

Festival performances have been known to catapult bands from the depths of obscurity to the bright lights of international fame and fortune – just look at Hot Chip (2006), Kate Nash (2007) and The Wombats (2008). Who'll be next? Hear them here first…

Truck Festival p106

Over 90 per cent of Truck Festival's performers are unsigned or at the very least signed to independent labels. Half the roster is made up of local bands, and through the years their unique takes on so many different genres – alternative indie, rock, folk and death metal – have excited hungry record label A&Rs. In essence, Robin and Joe Bennett (Truck's founders) are themselves successful A&Rs, scouting for unsigned talent at their favourite London venues, searching music websites or checking the online portal Sonicbids (which artists find is an easier alternative to posting demos). Seminally 'institutional' acts have graced Truck Festival's stages since it launched back in 1998, including: Maxïmo Park, Foals,

Do Me Bad Things, Get Cape. Wear Cape. Fly, Young Knives, Goldrush and Fell City Girl; and early appearances by the Editors and The Magic Numbers proved triumphant. Truck recently decided to focus even more attention to new talent by opening all six stages with unsigned bands, so you can now catch tomorrow's stars between 10am and midday every day for the duration of the festival. Already a firm favourite among those in the musical know, Truck Festival was the winner of the 2008 INDY Music Awards for best festival, receiving a special mention for their support of new and independent music.

music

end of the road   bestival

truck festival   offset

Sónar   p148

Barcelona's Sónar festival has excelled in devising quality music line-ups since 1999. Avant-garde experimental artists rub shoulders with electro superstars at numerous label showcases, arena shows and intimate gigs across the city. You can expect lashings of serious, very danceable late-night tunes mixed with a dash of irony (Jamie Cullum and Darren Emerson, anyone?) and soon-to-be-massive chart acts: Justice played here on a small stage returning, mid fame and fortune, to headline a main stage. The Soulwax/2 Many DJs duo were relatively unknown in Britain when they first played Sónar; while the Scissor Sisters launched their album to industry here in 2000 as unannounced special guests. Spanish authorities may have clamped down on the number of unofficial outdoor parties, but plenty of promoters manage to keep the Euro rave flowing in full swing, with after parties galore filling the city's nightclubs. Keeping the electronic sounds fresh, Sónar's spotters are out there hunting in unfamiliar territories (currently eastern Europe and Africa) as well as keeping an eye on the productive countries (Germany, Japan and Italy); if there's a new beat, they'll find it. No wonder Sónar is the destination of choice for jet-setting musos everywhere.

Offset   p70

The young people's festival, Offset is where you'll find London's glamorous twenty-somethings, into everything from their bright clothes and neon heels (the girls) to guyliner and manscara (the boys), when they're not walking the arty streets of Camden or Hackney. Over 190 bands of all shapes, calibres and sizes – playing artrock, indie, post-punk, rock, electro and increasing amounts of dubstep – supply enough revelationary music to keep these young style-setters enthused. Festival bookers scour the likes of Myspace and Twitter for interesting *au courant* artists, allocating them slots on one of the eight stages. Many *NME*-tipped, up-and-coming bands can be found here, and Offset's organisers whittle down 1,000-plus submissions to offer stage space to the 30 best new acts – recent winners include rising stars Ox.Eagle.Lion.Man, Underground Railroad and The Ghost Frequency. The festival runs its own music blog (www.thisisoffset.co.uk) tipping ones-to-watch, offering exclusive MP3s as well as promotional info for up-and-coming acts, encouraging a stream of new music and creating exposure for new artists. Club promoters such as Durrr, Trailer Trash and Club Artrocker ensure the late-night beats sound ultra-modern.

offset   sónar

End of the Road   p32

Simon Taffe loves music so much he gave up his job and mortgaged his house to start his own festival. As if that wasn't enough, he launched his own record label, too, and began using the festival to audition new bands for potential signage. This was how Woodpigeon band members found themselves signed to End of the Road Records in 2007 – having missed their performance, Simon arranged to meet eight of them at the piano tucked away in the woods, where, as soon as they had finished a cracker of an impromptu acoustic number, they were shaking hands over a new record deal. If Simon signs a band, surely it's going to be good, right? This is the man who booked Bon Iver, the Guillemots and Richard Hawley before the media caught wind of them and blew hype storms rolling over the British Isles. What's his secret – a crystal ball? Not really, he just listens to music every waking second of the day, and makes an annual pilgrimage to America's celebrated SXSW (South by South West) music convention where hopeful artists, record promoters and industry bods from all over the world gather in their thousands. Despite the festival's young age, End of the Road sells out fast – an affirmation, perhaps, that Simon was right to give up the day job.

Bestival   p22

Bestival always manages to allocate exactly the right musical soundtrack to whatever time of day, leaving no room for band overlaps or sudden changes in tempo (both of which can really upset an audience if handled badly). Privy to the best, hot new bands and up-and-coming acts (the legacy of the late, great broadcaster John Peel thrives with bands inundating Broadcasting House with their demos), Radio 1 DJ and Bestival co-founder, Rob da Bank, gets his mitts on the maddest, baddest beats months before release. An average week sees 400 CDs and 50 MP3s land on Rob's decks, but he's quick to pinpoint the ones likely to blow up (figuratively speaking, of course). Bestival was first off the block programming the likes of recent stars Mika, Sam Sparro, Kate Nash, Florence and The Machine, The Wombats and Friendly Fires. The BBC's stamp of approval went overground recently with their BBC Introducing...Stage, billing up-and-coming artists of a calibre rivalled only by the new Outdoor Stage in the 24 Hour Field. In actual fact, over half the acts treading all of this festival's stages are new bands. So confident is the Bestival team about its direction, it'll have two-dozen bands in the bag by the end of the year ready for the following summer.

estival   sōnar

BOOM✳

Boom sees itself as a 'lighthouse of sanity, ethical responsibility and a building block for the future to come'. Hifalutin claims perhaps, but they're backed up by 10 years' experience of bringing musicians, DJs, film-makers and speakers to a sustainable gathering of up to 30,000 people. With workshops ranging from art to yoga, 24-hour music, an underground film festival, a stunning lakeside location and the guaranteed sunshine of a Portuguese summer, it's hard not to be tempted by Boom's invitation to 'have fun, enjoy, open your perception channels, and enter'.

Music is spread across four stages. The Dancefloor belies Boom's trance roots, with an international line-up of DJs who are probably unknown beyond the psy-trance scene of Goa and Brazil. The Groovy Beach sound system has an equally international, yet equally unstarry line-up, with a more eclectic music policy that dabbles in reggae, funk and house, as well as hallucinogenic trance beats.

In the Ambient Forest, whooshing noises and serene soundscapes encourage the audience to sprawl across cushions. Relaxation is positively encouraged. Boom's recent addition is a Sacred Fire stage – a space for acoustic, world and folk music. Set in a purpose-built, hill-top garden, a welcome change of primal, earthy sounds greet anyone not into psy-trance.

Not that music is all that's on offer. Within the Liminal Village, permaculture gardens sit alongside multimedia installations – this is also the base for presentations, workshops, the film festival and a gallery. Luckily for the British visitor, many of the workshops, panels and films are in English. In fact, the international nature of the crowd (organisers estimate 70 per cent of the audience to be non-Portuguese) means language is rarely a barrier at Boom. In the Healing Area, tensions are rubbed away with massage, and *chakras* are tuned with Shamanic drumming, aura reading, sound healing and a dozen alternative offers to help you feel good.

In between the performance areas, dancefloors and workshop spaces, installation and walkabout artists ply their pictures, dances, sounds and words. A Baby Boom tent offers kiddy activities all day long and The Flea Market's crafts allow retail fans to peruse hand-made jewellery, craft items, tie-dye T-shirts and other 21st century hippy *objets d'art*.

There is a lot to do, learn and enjoy. But this is summer in Portugal where daytime temperatures can easily hit 35°C and over, so you probably won't want to do anything more frenetic than soak up some rays or seek out some shade. If it all gets too hot, then cool off with a refreshing dip in the beautiful lake.

The whole festival site emits a wonderfully spacious feel. This is true at the huge campsites too: there is plenty of room for comfy camping, a welcome change from the traditional festival squeeze. The communal kitchens (the risk of forest fires makes campfires illegal) and dozens of international food stalls, the abundance of drinkable water, showers and compost loos, free wi-fi Internet access, and of course, the weather, all add up to a great camping holiday.

As a festival location alone Boom is truly impressive. Combine that with its focus on recycling and bioconstruction (it speaks volumes about sustainable production), throw in an international line-up, plus a good-looking, open, alternative audience and you have one fantastic festival. Not just worthy of its place on the international psy-trance circuit – the four different stages feature world music, reggae, dub, dubstep, techno, house, breakbeat and ambient, too – Boom deserves a visit from any festival lover with horizons above and beyond the mainstream.

WHEN The festival happens every two years, to give the land and the organisers a breather, during the August full moon. It's next on in 2010.
GUIDE PRICE From €95 to €165.
CAPACITY 30,000
CAMPING The best views of the site are on the top of the hill overlooking the lake. There are showers and compost WCs all over the site, communal kitchens, a grocery store, and a camping area for caravans.
TOP TIP Catch a flight to anywhere in Portugal, Faro or Lisbon are best, then catch a Boom Bus, you'll reduce the carbon footprint.
LIKE THAT, THEN YOU'LL LOVE The Hove Festival (www.hovefestival.com) in Norway looks just as spectacular. Set in fern woodland overlooking the North Sea, it also promotes a strong environmental profile. Although tickets cost over twice as much as Boom, the bands who play here are huge.
LOCATION Herdade do Torrão, Idanha-a-Nova, Portugal

www.boomfestival.org

In the late '70s, when disco was ruling the Western world, Yugoslavia's nightlife consisted of live gigs and 'igranka' dance halls where local bands would play covers of traditional Italian songs. Nightclubs eventually started popping up in the basements and grounds of hotels, but their atmosphere was light years behind New York's trailblazing disco culture.

In the mid-'80s a handful of Croatians returned from Germany – the biggest host nation for Yugoslav migrant workers – equipped with vinyl singles and Technics DJ decks. Club culture was finally surfacing; and by the end of the decade, Eurovision-style pop and obligatory Italo Disco (popular in southern Europe) could be heard pounding out of most main city nightclubs.

After the civil war had divvied old Yugoslavia into individual states, a wave of modern house music enveloped the Croatian music scene. Incurring denunciations from the Church about the 'devil music', young Croats celebrated the ceasefire at open-air raves and in underground car parks, stopping only when police would swoop in and switch off the generators.

Fast-forward to the end of this decade and Croatia's dance scene is in a healthy place. A number of clubs in the capital, Zagreb, now stage Ibizan-style residencies along the Dalmatian Coast. And north of Zadar, Barbarella's nightclub hosts a number of Brit-centric festivals. Hidden inside the woods on the Pinija peninsula, this indoor–outdoor venue was closed during the war before being taken over by refugees. These days it's owned by two Brummies, Nick Colgan and Eddie O'Callaghan. The duo stripped away the paint, unearthing original Italian architecture, and keeping the 1970s feel very much intact, they installed top of the range sound systems, restored three bars (including a wonderful circular *Tiki* cocktail bar with sea views) and dotted the outdoor areas with huge plants.

The Electric Elephant festival is the pride and joy of Manchester's DJ darlings, the Unabombers. Emulating Colgan's own festival at Barbarella's, The Garden, they launched the first Electric Elephant here in 2008. With the sea lapping at the decking as the party dances under a setting sun, the setting is as idyllic as it gets.

The weekend featured DJs from midday, followed by a host of live music (incorporating dubstep to acoustic folk) at the outdoor beach bar and terrace. Anyone fast enough to get tickets could extend the festivities by hopping aboard one of the boat parties hosted by disco doyens Electric Chair, Horse Meat Disco and

Low Life. Then from 1am, everyone ends up in the basement club, where a sea of sun-kissed arms wave in the air until 6am.

The festival was so sociable that word is already out, but future events will cater for the inevitable increase in numbers. More boat parties (tickets will be sold in advance to allow everyone a chance to set sail, as happens at The Garden Festival in July), more live music, an extended beach bar and possibly a floating dancefloor are several new touches being planned, and the parties will run from Thursday to Monday. Of course, the Unabombers will continue their reign as the diverse daddies of Dalmatian dance and will programme the type of DJs and live bands that compliment and echo their own dancefloor beliefs: soul, house, funk, folk, hip-hop, rock, jazz and electronica.

Croatia is easy to travel to and around. Cheap airlines fly to Zadar and Split, buses run from the airport to Zadar and from there to Petrčane, or you can pick up a taxi or hire car at the airport or town centre (contact numbers are handed out in the festival's information packs). The climate is great, the coastline is stunning and the atmosphere at this festival...Well, it's electric of course.

WHEN End August
GUIDE PRICE Tickets £70; £5 per boat party.
CAPACITY 2,000
CAMPING Camp Pineta is a basic, family-run campsite in Petrčane, down the road from Barbarella's, that fits in 30 tents (Punta Radmana 21, 23223 Petrčane, Hrvatska; www.camp-pineta.com). No noise allowed after 11pm!
TOP TIP Take a break from the non-stop revelry and hire a car to explore the country. The nearest cash point is a long, steep walk out of Petrčane, so pre-order the car to arrive halfway through the week when you'll need more cash. Some companies will even deliver a car to your accommodation. Watch out for undercover policemen, too, Croatia has a zero tolerance policy on drugs.
LIKE THAT, THEN YOU'LL LOVE The Garden Festival (www.thegardenfestival.eu), also at Barbarella's. Parties run across two weekends in July, with stuff going on during the week, too. It attracts a younger crowd and the house music is some of the best you'll hear all summer (£70 for a three-day festival pass or £120 for both weekends). The 25,000-capacity INmusic festival (www.inmusicfestival.com/en) in June is by the beautiful Jarun lake in Zagreb. Past artists have included Nick Cave, Iggy Pop & The Stooges and The Prodigy.
LOCATION Punta Radman, Petrčane, Zadar, Croatia, 23231

www.electricelephant.co.uk

Electric Picnic

The journey to Electric Picnic starts with a bit of a shock. That is one pricey ticket! Does this make it the most expensive festival in Europe? We're not sure but our expectations are raised; we're hoping for a 5-star weekend.

As you arrive at Stradbally, an hour's drive from Dublin, you'll be directed to car parks that border the main arena. So with enough forward planning and know-how you can arrange to camp with your friends without having to trek for miles laden like a pack mule. Result.

All the campsites have their own personalities. The tree-lined Oscar Wilde camping area houses the Dance Village and the only ATM, which means it tends to be noisy and busy at night. Jimi Hendrix is closest to the festival arena, the late-night Body & Soul hangout and the Village Green. Charlie Chaplin overlooks the comedy, spoken word and theatre enclosures, while Andy Warhol, the furthest away, is quieter and calmer. Families have their own campsite sensibly positioned at the south-eastern end of the site away from the late-night revelry, next to a lake, an enchanting walled garden full of apples and cider, and a magical kiddies' wonderland.

So far, so 5-star. A walk through the woods hints at what's in store. A big pirate ship looms out of the trees; its massive hull is an unexpected, amusing spectacle. Further along the path, bass-heavy reggae booms out of a sound system, it looks like there's a band playing among the branches. Finally, you pass through a wrist-band and alcohol check and step into complete sensory overload. There are just so many stages, sound systems, cabarets, tents, bandstands, bars, cafés, food stalls, installations and decorations in every direction that you'll find your head spins in utter bewilderment. In a good way.

Musically, the line-up dominates your journey as household (or soon to be) names are crammed into a timetable you'll want to keep tabs on. In 2008, thousands fell under Grace Jones' rhythmic spell, (later crowned Mercury-winners) Elbow raised the roof, and acts such as Franz Ferdinand, George Clinton, Underworld, Duffy, Crystal Castles, Santogold and Tindersticks performed. That was just three hours, at a fraction of the stages, in one single evening.

The spoken-word programme brought theatre, storytelling, stand-up, literature, debate and poetry to spoken word tents and a huge Comedy Club tent. Other than the latter, which was packed, these tents didn't look too busy during the day. Eyes and ears were obviously too bewitched by the random large-scale installations; especially the fire-breathing, smoke-belching, water-spouting Arcadia sound system. Amazing!

A massive circus arena was a novel draw for anyone who'd not seen clowns and trapeze artists since childhood. Then there were the: Lost Vagueness Asylum, Silent Disco, Dance Village, cinema, World Music stage, Pussy Parlure, Little Big Tent, Salty Dog Saloon, Temple of Truth, Crawdaddy stage, Inflatable Church, Maypole, Granny's Gaff, Cider Bar, Amnesty Tea and Bingo Hall, Human Jukebox, Teas and Tarts, not forgetting the herd of topiary elephants. The list goes on and on and on.

What band to see, where to sit, where to wander next? It's almost a relief to relax late at night in the amazing Body & Soul area illuminated by magical tree lights. In the centre is a hollow bowl that's filled with dancers bopping away until the early hours.

Everyone at Ireland's leading eclectic weekend is totally up for the *craic*. Despite the initial shock then, the answer is yes, it is excellent value for money.

WHEN Late August/early September
GUIDE PRICE Approximately €220 for a weekend ticket.
CAPACITY 30,000
CAMPING Various camping areas are named after cultural icons (Oscar Wilde, Charlie Chaplin, Jimi Hendrix, Andy Warhol). You can buy burgers, nachos and hotdogs in some of the campsites and one of them boasts a modern supermarket bigger than your average local village store.
TOP TIP Everyone is super-friendly and while it's boozy at night it isn't overly hedonistic. Get there when the gates open and stay until the very end, you won't want to miss a thing. In 2008 the multi-flashing LED-lit Quad Cubatron and America's Burning Man legend, David Best, and his burning Temple of Truth were spellbounding.
LIKE THAT, THEN YOU'LL LOVE Take a cheap flight to Budapest and check out the madly creative Sziget (p192).
LOCATION Stradbally Hall Estate, Stradbally, Co. Laois, Republic of Ireland

www.electricpicnic.com

If you're looking for a party then you've come to the right place. At Exit's fairy-tale fortress kingdom, you will find yourself in the company of countrymen who danced their way to freedom and will probably party for eternity.

Generally, most countries experiencing the throes of serious political upset will harbour a flourishing underground dance scene. Exit festival was borne out of a 1999 student protest that rallied in opposition to the Milošević regime. When Serbian students staged a 100-day sit-in, it quickly turned into a 100-day-long party. On the very last day, the Exit crew sent a message to the world by marching from Novi Sad to Belgrade, joining a 500,000-strong gathering that called for the expulsion of the dictator Slobodan Milošević after a disputed presidential election. Defeated by so many protestors, Milošević fell from his National Assembly perch and the course of the country's leadership was changed forever.

Serbians now celebrate this moment every year, at what has become one of the best-publicised live music and dance events on the European circuit – Exit. Although the party lasts for just a fraction of the original protest, visitors can squeeze an awful lot of quality music and fun fringe activities into these four days, without the added worry of having a dictator to topple.

Looking out of the clock tower of the 18th-century Austro-Hungarian Petrovaradin Fortress, the city of Novi Sad and the River Danube twinkle below. Stone walls, ramparts, tunnels and old lantern lamps line the cobbled streets within and outside the fortress walls. Daylight recovery hours are usually spent hanging out at The Strand, a section of the river where you can swim. It also has a bar where you can start the evening with a drink before heading to the main arena when the real fun starts.

In the walk up to the entrance, festival goers are tempted to buy cheap beer, unofficial merchandise and are cajoled into trying the local, lethal booze, *rakija*, for a couple of euros. Onsite, there are stalls selling food, official merchandise, a variety of souvenirs and artwork, and many of the festival essentials – phone top-up cards, sun cream and bottled water.

Musically, Exit is bang on the money: a whole load of well-known bands, cutting-edge DJs and visual artists provide one of the most adventurous, energetic live playlists you're likely to hear all summer. This is a meeting of rock to rap and classical to popular à la mode music that has so far included all sorts of acts from Snoop Dogg to Franz Ferdinand, Basement Jaxx and Iggy Pop. Among the whopping 16 stages there is a chill-out space and a cinema, but this is Exit we're talking about, home of the (100 days and nights) hardcore, so you should expect to see most of the audience on their feet, their arms in the air, for most of the night.

Many airlines fly to central Belgrade, and from there it is an hour's drive to Novi Sad. You can park near to the camping areas (head to the warehouse reception to exchange your tickets for wristbands). If you prefer using public transport, jump on one of the buses running from the airport to Belgrade and from there you can catch a train to Novi Sad.

Exit is well worth the journey. The festival has blossomed into a powerful symbol of freedom enjoyed by many visiting Europeans because of its distinctive cultural, historic uniqueness. Exit embraces positivity, tolerance and a sense of community – everything, in fact, that a genuine festival ought to promote.

WHEN Early July
GUIDE PRICE €72 for four days, €20–30 per day and an additional €14 to camp.
CAPACITY 35,000 daily
CAMPING You can pitch up just a 30-minute walk from the festival site in the University Park, by the River Danube. Exit is a night-time festival so everyone tends to relax at the campsite or by the river by day, heading to the fortress later in the evening.

By the river, there's a lifeguard keeping a watchful eye on the swimmers and an Exit shop that sells camping equipment. Officials patrol regularly to ensure the safety and security of campers at all times.
TOP TIP Pace yourself with the booze, the party lasts all through the night and until the morning, so you won't want to peak too early.
LIKE THAT, THEN YOU'LL LOVE If you want to test your stamina in true Exit style (in other words, you want to party for days and days) then the longest event in Europe could be the 10-day electronic music event that is 10 Days Off (www.10daysoff.be/uk) in Ghent, Belgium, which also takes place in July.
LOCATION Petrovaradin Fortress, Novi Sad, Serbia

German festivals: all Kraftwerk techno, Love Parades and huge Stein glasses of beer? Jeez, no, when was the last time you visited Berlin? While techno is still holding its own as a prime movement of the underground, plenty of edgier music scenes have gradually been taking over from the sharp bleeps and heavy beats.

It's not just Germany's capital that's currently bursting with style; the country is also home to Melt! festival. Set in Ferropolis (or the 'City of Steel' as it's otherwise known) the site houses a collection of unused 20th-century machinery that, when lit up at night, takes on the appearance of a futuristic *Mad Max* film set.

Although the weather has the potential to be shocking (as it was in 2008), a festival that's surrounded by towering, sky-high, old rusting excavators won't allow its reputation to be tainted by a drop of rain. And with such a unique setting, you could be forgiven for thinking that Melt!'s bosses could just roll out the techno then sit back and watch their tickets sell out. They don't, though. This is a festival where over 100 acts and DJs play more electronica, in all of its glorious forms, than anything else.

If there's no space left in the standing area in front of the main Medusa Stage, set within a concrete pit, audiences can get a great view of the acts from the surrounding tiers of steps. As night falls, the whole place turns into a dystopian *wunderland* as swooping *Batman*-style searchlights, screeching fireworks and strobes light up the sky like a scene from an animated science fiction film – totally trippy.

In the Melt!Klub Room and the Museum Room, prepare to be blasted by the force of hip-hop, grime, dubstep, indie and rock. Yes, the line-up has had a slight British bent to date, with Kate Nash and Franz Ferdinand among recent performers, but this has been welcomed by the ever-increasing number of British expats living in Berlin. The journey to this 20,000-capacity event isn't much more that an hour's drive from Berlin or you can take the train to either Dessau or Gräfenhainichen.

Melt!'s statistics report that 80 per cent of attendees are under 30, which might explain why you'll see thousands of eager beavers at the gates waiting for them to open. Melt! protocol sees these young 'uns planting themselves by a stage (there are five in total, indoor and out) where they'll stay put until the sound systems are switched off, signalling the end of the night. Across the grass there's a quarry filled with water, forming an artificial lake where people can swim during the day.

Refreshment-wise the nation's favourite – sausages – can be devoured along with anything from Turkish kebabs or sushi to burgers and chips. Naturally, beer is a big intoxicator here, German brands are sold all over the 1950s urban sprawl and bottles of Prosecco also do a roaring trade.

Melt! is the kind of festival where the audience completely engages with the artists, who, in turn, work even harder to maintain the atmosphere's heady buzz of excitement. For those Germans who've only had a limited range of rock events on offer in the past, Melt! is positively pioneering. With beautiful, trendy, style popcorn; pounding sound systems ringing out like klaxons; screeching fireworks setting the night sky alight and searchlights sweeping overhead, you'll find yourself caught up in a Ferropolis fantasy world you won't want to wake from until you're on the plane heading back home.

WHEN Mid July

GUIDE PRICE From €45 for a day pass, €70 for 2 days and €90 for 3 days.

CAPACITY 20,000

CAMPING Opposite the industrial site is an overgrown, grassy, wild camping spot on the Gremmin Lake. There is a supermarket open 24 hours a day. Fancy campers can hire three-bed tents with Jacuzzi, breakfast and a nearby post office. Otherwise you can pay to sleep in a pre-erected tent (see website for details).

TOP TIP Prolong your holiday with a stay at the very unusual, slightly scruffy-around-the-edges, but superbly positioned 125-pitch campsite, Tentstation (www.tentstation.de) as featured in *Cool Camping: Europe*, just 10 minutes from Berlin city centre.

LIKE THAT, THEN YOU'LL LOVE Well you might not love this one quite as much, but if you like your festivals to be bigger and bolder, then all roads lead to Rock am Ring and Rock im Park (www.rock-am-ring.de) that take place in west and south east Germany over one weekend in early June.

LOCATION Ferropolis – 'City of Steel', Ferropolisstraße 1, 06773 Gräfenhainichen, Germany

www.meltfestival.de

BRIGHT YOUNG THINGS

Whether you're a worldly 14-year-old who enjoys live music or an 18-year-old who likes partying all night, festivals are just brilliant. The music, the bands, the lifestyle – everything justifies an excuse to let loose and have fun. In nightclubs everybody tends to know one another and that can inhibit people's behaviour – so being outdoors in the countryside offers a freedom that can't be beaten. In recent years, there's been this 'festivalisation' of live music that has seen a huge surge of events popping up all over the place, in fields, parks and cities...Increasingly, promoters are hosting all-inclusive ticket affairs where you get a wristband and can watch 20 or so bands playing in a dozen different venues in just one evening. London has a really good festival aimed solely at 18s and under, called Underage. It offers teenagers who are into style, music and fashion an alternative place to hang out to the 'normal' festivals. Fashion among today's youth is different and unique; they wear skinny jeans and cut their hair into big lofty fringes. Teenagers are as devoted to chasing new bands as generations before them, if not more so. Favourite festivals for today's youth will be Reading (p72) – for the sheer scale of the crowd and all those guitars – and Offset (p70) because it features so much new music.

STEVE SLOCOMBE
CREATIVE DIRECTOR, *SUPERSUPER*

Only the clean-living, well-disciplined Swiss could pull off one of the biggest and longest award-winning, open-air festivals in Europe, year after year, and run it entirely on sustainable energy.

Paléo's evolution has been a remarkable one. Beginning life indoors in 1976 as the First Folk Festival, it emerged into the sunlight the following year with a new title, the Nyon Folk Festival. There was one more name change (to Paléo Festival Nyon) before it spread its wings in 1990 and moved to its current 84-hectare grassy home between Geneva and Lausanne.

Organisers estimate that their audience is mostly comprised of Swiss-French visitors. And as Switzerland signs up most of its men for compulsory military service training, this might explain why the behaviour of the crowd is, on the whole, pleasantly dignified. Even if the vibe is more rock than roll, Paléo needn't be written off as a pedestrian affair. It should be embraced for its creative qualities and strong environmental purpose; the festival is entirely powered by sustainable energy, using electricity converted from Alps' wind and water energy.

A stay here is as refreshing as the alpine breezes sweeping in from those nearby mountains. You're in the company of an audience that considers moral and music standards to be more important than grabbing their next malt and hops fix. Oasis once upset the crowd so much with a lacklustre performance that a barrage of cans and coins were lobbed onto the stage: cue the band's hasty retreat. In other words, if you like to watch skilled, passionate musicians in chilled, calm, beautiful surroundings, then Paléo is your kind of festival.

The music line-up is released every April. Well-known, home-grown talent is thin on the ground (Switzerland's never really made its mark on the international musical map) but Paléo makes up for it by booking international stadium rock gods alongside unknown French-singing groups and Indian world music legends, such as the legendary sitar player, Ravi Shankar, who put on an unforgettable performance at Paléo's 30th anniversary in 2005.

As at most festivals nowadays, there's much more than music to amuse the masses. Rooting around for distractions here is no lengthy task. Six stages,164 performers, over 4,000 volunteers (Paléo is a non-profit-making organisation), hundreds of food and craft stalls, five restaurants, a club tent, a day nursery and a children's play area (see also p121) give an idea of the tremendous scope on offer. It's not surprising that this event sells out so quickly.

You can indulge your more exotic fantasies and energetic whims at La Ruche, a huge section dedicated to circus, cabaret and street theatre. Each year, the Village du Monde showcases food and music from a different part of the world (in 2009 it's India). In addition to the Latin and Oriental Areas the festival's food selection – hot spicy curry, couscous, raclette – will take your tastebuds on a culinary journey to anywhere in the world.

The atmosphere is fired with genteel enthusiasm and facilities are family-friendly. Getting here is easy too with free transportation from nearby towns, surrounding villages and Nyon train station. And get this for sensible festival prep – the website suggests that friends should decide in advance who'll be driving the car home and draw up a contract, Le Contrat de Confiance, which the driver can then swap for an apple juice on arrival. Whether or not this will catch on in the UK is dubious, but you heard it here first.

Switzerland may well be up to its mountain-tops in Lindt chocolate, but the winning beauty regime of fresh, alpine air and free-flowing spring water attributes to a general fresh-faced allure. In other words, be prepared for your first ever bout of skin envy, you'll be mingling among the clearest complexions in Europe.

WHEN Late July
GUIDE PRICE Ranging from approximately €33 for a day to €180 for six days.
CAPACITY 35,000 daily
CAMPING Campsites open on the Monday before the event starts, closing the following Monday. Most people only camp for two or three nights. There's room for 7,000 campers at any one time, on flat land (unlike the festival site, which is sloping in areas). To help you find your tent, the camping field is divided into streets named after cities or countries (Singapore, Peking, New York and so on), with information points situated either side of the entrance to the festival to help you should you lose your way.
TOP TIP Named after a famous 1970s racehorse Paléo may be, but you'll need the stamina of an ox to survive the six-day lifespan. Recycling and waste disposal is of paramount importance – having won a MIDEM Green World Award (2008), Paléo has pretty high standards to uphold.
LIKE THAT, THEN YOU'LL LOVE Since 1967 the Montreux Jazz Festival (www.montreuxjazz.com), on the shores of Lake Geneva, has always featured some of the most prodigious jazz, soul and blues greats from around the world. Recently, organisers have included contemporary pop acts on the bill as the old jazz greats are sadly a dying breed.
LOCATION Route de St-Cergue 312, CP 1320, CH-1260 Nyon 1, Switzerland

www.paleo.ch

There was a moment at Pukkelpop in 2008 when, as the crowd were losing their minds in one of the massive 5,000-capacity plastic air hangars, something quite incredible happened. A man in a wheelchair was lifted above the sweaty throng and, helped by the audience, he crowd-surfed (still in his wheelchair) all the way to the front. It was a heavenly image that will endure for many years to come.

The site is an airfield in a country where 'flat terrain' is a geographical understatement. Few natural wonders beautify the site apart from enormous trees that prettily chaperone the main stage. Dressing up the site's plain aesthetics, an abundance of colourful flags blow everywhere. While the camping ground is a little bit gritty, the food is common festival fare (although, like most European festivals, drinks and food are bought with a token system, speeding up service) and mobile phone banners and corporate emblems are everywhere, ultimately, this is all irrelevant to the loyal fans.

One of the reasons why bands such as Daft Punk, Radiohead and Metallica have headlined here over the past few years is because of the high-spirited audience. Belgians aren't as subdued as they're reputed to be. Young crowds saunter around, bouncing between stages and cinemas to the Petit Bazar cultural village (to watch comedians), the Moroccan village (to sip tea), the champagne bar (well that one's obvious) and the Belgian beer tent (it'd be rude not to) bent on savouring every single moment.

The fancy dress factor common to UK festivals is kept to a minimum and 'glamping' *accoutrements* are equally non-existent. All that's left is a crowd, a crowd loving the music and the music loving them back.

WHEN Mid/late August
GUIDE PRICE Weekend tickets are approximately €135.
CAPACITY 152,000
CAMPING You can pitch up opposite the festival site. It can be quite noisy with the French- and German-Belgians locked in verbal friendly fire till late, but quieter spots can be found if you arrive early. There are areas for hanging out or cooking and a second-hand shop sells camping gear.
TOP TIP Spend some time in the dance tent. An incredible production, screens drop down from the ceiling as fast-moving green LED lights dart across the arena. Also, Hasselt centre is the so-called Belgian 'Capital of Good Taste', full of shops and restaurants, so it's worth a visit.
LIKE THAT, THEN YOU'LL LOVE Dour (www.dourfestival.be/en) by name, friendly by nature, the dance-to-alt-indie-pop fest merges the old with the new next to a lake in a disused quarry.
LOCATION Kempische Steenweg, 3500 Kiewit-Hasselt, Belgium

ROSKILDE

This festival places camping right at the heart of the fun. Four 'warm up' days of music and activities take place in the 80-hectare campsite, where, from the Sunday to the Wednesday, up-and-coming Scandinavian bands perform at the Pavilion Junior mini stage, and elsewhere other activities such as BMX and skating spectacles are laid on. All this, before the actual festival has even begun.

Created in 1971, Roskilde is situated 20 miles to the west of Copenhagen in Denmark. It's one heck of a behemoth, but has the requisite infrastructure to cope. Back in the '70s the Danish music scene was dominated by folk bands, so the folk stage used to be a popular draw. Now it's primarily a rock festival, with world, rap and electronica music played in equal measure. Artists and designers spruce up the site with various art installations and creative designs so it doesn't look or feel like a big money-making machine.

Actually, the festival is now run by The Roskilde Festival Charity Society, and donates all profits to different humanitarian and cultural causes each year. More than 25,000 volunteers play a part in creating a special, non-corporate vibe. And you can't get more anti-corporate than a nude running competition; midday on Saturday is when student radio stations stage a race in which around 30 people take part in male and female heats, with the winners awarded a free festival ticket.

The campsite even has its own train station linking you to Copenhagen Central Station and Copenhagen Airport, and shuttle buses run between the site and Roskilde's centre every 15 minutes. This has made it even simpler for more and more Germans, Australians and us Brits to travel to this great big Danish party with ease.

WHEN Early July (first weekend) but the campsite warm up starts at the end of June.
GUIDE PRICE Tickets are for the whole week and cost approximately £200. Children's tickets are about £102 (and are only sold at the gates).
CAPACITY 110,000
CAMPING People make up their own themes for the campsite areas, which are divided into sections, and prizes are awarded for the best. Die-hard partiers camp at the northern part of camping East. Facilities include showers, communal grills, food and drink stalls, shopping areas, cinema, skate ramp and free luggage storage.
TOP TIP Denmark is the home of bacon, so hunt down the *brændende kærlighed* (burning love) dish, which consists of mashed potatoes with fried bacon, garnished with parsley.
LIKE THAT, THEN YOU'LL LOVE The Hultsfred Festival (www.rockparty.se) in Sweden is a smaller rock and pop event.
LOCATION Festivalpladsen, Darupvej 19, DK-4000 Roskilde, Denmark

www.roskilde-festival.dk

Sziget is Hungarian for 'island' and no prizes for guessing where this Eastern European wonder world takes place. That's right, on an island in Hungary! Ok, Óbudai Island to be more precise, which is Budapest's most northerly island on the River Danube. Given the huge size of the site, other than when you're crossing the bridge over the river, most of the time you'll think you're in a leafy country park rather than a bustling Eastern European city.

Sziget was devised by a group of musician friends in 1993 after the fall of Communism and it has grown into one of Europe's definitive rock festivals. Temperatures sizzle at an average 30°C in August, as the climate becomes more Mediterranean by the year. However, given the vagaries of the weather, as at all festivals, do go prepared for both sun and showers.

The site is approximately half the size of Monaco, so building it is no mean feat. It takes 6,000 people two weeks to put stages and entertainment areas together, in all kinds of configurations, for more than 1,000 artists to churn out metal, rock, African, Latin, jazz, dance and world music to some 340,000 visitors. During the week there's plenty of space to spread out, but weekends are a tighter squeeze when the locals pour in to see the headline acts.

During these peak times the footfall in and out of the island rises significantly (they have security checkpoints searching bags and checking wristbands) and it can get quite busy at key junctions in between acts. Ideally, leave enough time to travel between destinations as there are so many things to see and distract you along the way. Signs at major junctions point the way towards different areas, and handy pocket size maps help to keep you on track.

On Day Zero, the first day of the festival, the show starts with a big bang by way of a mega artist or comeback gig, which in previous years has included the Sex Pistols and Iron Maiden. The ensuing line-up is a who's who of indie and rock. A Theatre and Dance Tent flies in choreographers from as far a field as Cuba and Japan, while further cultural entertainment showcases drama, puppetry, contemporary dance, fine art, ballet and poetry. There's a Roma Tent where you can practise your hip-shaking gypsy moves, and the omnipresent dance Party Arena stays open until 5am.

Extra attractions include a cinema, games consoles, tennis, football, swimming, abseiling, archery, bungee jumping, zip-lining, err...wet T-shirt competitions, foam parties, henna and ink tattooing, Thai massages and lots of other holistic, hippy happenings, too. Phew! Throw in campsites, showers and a travelling funfair and it's like living in a children's fantasy holiday camp, sound-tracked by the best music in the world. A huge variety of food to tempt all palates is cooked up – from Western European basics to Hungarian cuisine, including barbecued and roasted meats seasoned with paprika (the national seasoning of choice) and delicious Lángos pastries.

German is the second language of many Hungarians, so go armed with a few key words to impress your affable hosts; but if you're not a linguist don't worry, almost everyone speaks English at the festival; and a smile will more than often suffice. The *New York Times* once wrote of the line-up, 'Sziget functions less as a music festival than as a kind of small-scale United Nations'. Though there's little chance of spotting Kofi Annan among the crowd, this festival does have a very cosmopolitan feel to it. While Hungary has moved its economy forward since joining the EU, the average disposable income is much less than in Western Europe, and so with the entry ticket for the week costing up to €180, it's no surprise that the crowd at this Hungarian adventure is comprised of a global commingle of nationalities.

WHEN Early/mid August
GUIDE PRICE Daily ticket €40; advance week ticket without camping from €120; with camping from €150.
CAPACITY 340,000
CAMPING There's room for 30,000 campers so the key is to arrive as early as possible (check out the official website to find out when the gates open). Pitch your tent as far away from the heavy metal tent as you can; peaceful spots are located at the northern tip of the island. Moderate facilities are onsite and a hypermarket with cash points and a pharmacy is 1km away. For all other supplies, Budapest centre is a 20-minute tram ride away.
TOP TIP If you're desperate for a hot shower, you can always head off to the Lido on Margit Island, where, for the price of a day ticket, you can swim, sunbathe and shower afterwards. Definitely fit in some sightseeing of the main Budapest sites and travel from the centre by ferry to pass the (floodlit at night) Buda Castle, Chain Bridge and Margit Island on Danube's coastline.
LIKE THAT, THEN YOU'LL LOVE England's Glastonbury (p42) is the only other festival offering as much cultural variety on this scale.
LOCATION Budapest 1033, Óbudai sziget, Május 9. park , Hungary

WORLDWIDE FESTIVAL

Every July a glamorous cast of European fans descend upon the sleepy Mediterranean fishing town of Sète. Framed by beautiful ocean views and situated just a half hour train ride from Montpellier, this picturesque port plays host to the beats-and-bass-heavy Worldwide Festival.

Since Worldwide's emergence onto the festival scene, many of the headline performances at the 2,000-capacity Theatre de la Mer have been nothing short of jaw dropping. Behind this amphitheatre's stage gigantic trawlers and small boats glide past, then, as the sun slips away over the horizon, musical luminaries play out the parting rays with style and panache.

Once the evening has cooled down, everyone re-groups down the road at Base Nautique. A good-looking industrial space, it is situated in the heart of Sète's harbour, guarded by a majestic lighthouse. At night it's transformed into an outdoor, old-school rave complete with a stage, bar and Funktion-One sound system. Laurent Garnier and host Gilles Peterson are regular DJs. When the sun rises, darting pink candy hues across the skies, it's time for everyone to catch up on their sleep.

Come midday the party is literally back on its feet over on the eight-mile-long beach on the Triangle de Villeroy, where various coves offer privacy for danced-out souls to relax in peace between bouts of bopping and snacking at the ACD beach bar-restaurant. Time flies, and before long it's all aboard the shuttle bus for the five-minute ride back to the amphitheatre where more big band entertainment awaits.

With an ambitious wish-list that includes Seu Jorge, Rufus Wainwright, Talib Kweli, Kate Bush and Radiohead, Worldwide looks set to continue its reign as king of the leftfield festivals.

WHEN First weekend in July
GUIDE PRICE €100–110 four-day pass.
CAPACITY 2,000 for the Theatre de la Mer and Nautical Base, and 10,000 for the beach party (ACD Plage).
CAMPING There are 384 tent pitches at the family campsite Le Castellas (www.le-castellas.com/en), which is 20 metres from the beach, but a 10-mile trek from the festival, so you'll need to hire a vehicle to come and go.
TOP TIP Pack a pair of flats along with your heels for the cobbled walk, ladies. And be sure to dance yourselves up an appetite – over 80 restaurants in town serve fresh monkfish, mussels, stuffed squids and other fresh catches.
LIKE THAT, THEN YOU'LL LOVE Calvi on the Rocks (www.calviontherocks.com) in Corsica is a must for anyone seeking paradisiacal swimming with four nights of electronic, punk-funk. Or, Lyon's Nuits Sonores (www.nuits-sonores.com) is an electronic and indie affair in May.
LOCATION Theatre de la Mer/ Base Nautique/ACD Plage, Sète, France

5 festivals

good for...

acknowledgements

The Cool Camping Guide to Festivals

Series Concept & Series Editor: Jonathan Knight

Researched and written by: Sam Pow

Project Manager: Nikki Sims

Editors: Sophie Dawson, Nikki Sims

Proofreader: Jessica Cowie

Design and artwork: Kenny Grant

Picture Research: Kenny Grant, Polly Hall and Sam Pow

PR: The Farley Partnership

Published by: Punk Publishing, 3 The Yard, Pegasus Place, London SE11 5SD

Distributed by: Portfolio Books, Suite 3/4 Great West House, Great West Road, Brentford, Middlesex TW8 9DF

The publishers and authors have done their best to ensure the accuracy of all information in *The Cool Camping Guide to Festivals*, however, they can accept no responsibility for any injury, loss, or inconvenience sustained by anyone as a result of information contained in this book.

All information was correct at the time of going to press.

Sam Pow would like to thank the following: Writers/contributors/tippers: Chris Salmon, Craig McLean (for last minute Franz help, too), Julian Hall, Phil Meadley and Simon Kelly. Rui Teimao, Rob Dabrowski, Dan Davies, Sarah Hay, Karen Young, Carl Loben, Greg Lowe, Rida Attarashany, Sarah Kingsbury and Fiona Cartledge. Thanks also to all the festival organisers and their PRs, especially Alex Lee Thomson, Dani Cotter, Duncan Turner and Romain Gomis; every photographer who donated pictures (a donation will be made to The Photographer's Gallery) and the Punk Publishing dream team Sophie Dawson, Kenny Grant, Jonathan Knight and Nikki Sims.

Insider Insight extracts: page 95 taken from *Class of 88: The True Acid House Experience* (Anniversary Edition) by Wayne Anthony; page 151 taken from: *Nirvana: The True Story* (Omnibus Press) by Everett True.

We hope you've enjoyed this book and that it's inspired you to get your tickets, pack your tent and head off to a field somewhere. The festivals featured are a personal selection chosen by Sam Pow and the Punk Publishing team. None of the festivals has paid a fee for inclusion, so you can be sure of an objective choice of festivals and frank, honest descriptions. Peace Out.